CHILDREN'S FEARS

OF WAR AND

TERRORISM

A RESOURCE FOR
TEACHERS AND PARENTS

Lisa F. Moses
Florence City Schools, Alabama
Jerry Aldridge
University of Alabama at Birmingham
Anarella Cellitti
University of Alabama al Birmingham
Gwenyth McCorquodale
University of Alabama at Birmingham

Association for Childhood Education International

Anne W. Bauer, ACEI Editor
Bruce Herzig, ACEI Editor

Library of Congress Cataloging-in-Publication Data
Children's fears of war and terrorism : a resource for teachers and
parents / Lisa F. Moses ... [et al.].
    p. cm.
Includes bibliographical references.
  ISBN 0-87173-160-6 (pbk.)
1. Children and war. 2. War--Psychological aspects. 3.
Terrorism--Psychological aspects. 4. Fear in children. 5. Emotional
problems of children. I. Moses, Lisa F.

 BF723.W3C48 2003
 155.4'1246--dc21
                              2003011040

TABLE OF CONTENTS

PREFACE

Collectively, the four of us have taught for over 100 years. We have witnessed many changes in the world that affect children, but none so striking as the increased concerns and fears children are expressing over war and terrorism. We remember being children ourselves and living under the threat of nuclear war; we remember being told to hide under our desks at school, as if that would protect us from an atomic bomb. However, at that time we did not have 24-hour-a-day news coverage on television that constantly bombarded us with images of war and discussions of terrorism.

We developed this book through a desire to help children deal with their fears related to armed conflict and terrorist attacks. Because the Association for Childhood Education International is an international organization, we have worked hard to make the book accessible to the global community. Nevertheless, three of us have lived our entire lives in the southeastern United States, and our backgrounds cannot help but shine through in these pages.

Organization of the Book

This book provides an introduction to children's fears related to war and terrorism. The key word here is "fears." Much can be said about armed conflicts, but here we have limited our scope to fears. The first chapter covers the background and history of children's fears. The second chapter addresses the impact of context on these fears. Chapter Three considers the influence of temperament, while Chapter Four reviews the importance of the child's age when dealing with fears concerning war or terrorism. Chapters Five and Six explore ways teachers and parents can help children cope with their fears through children's literature and aesthetic experiences. Finally, the Epilogue deals with the complexities adults face in helping children work through their fears.

While all four of us have vastly different views about some of the issues associated with war and terrorism, we do have one thing in common. We are committed to helping all children work through their fears and anxieties related to threats of war and acts of terrorism. We hope this book will help you make a difference in the lives of children in the uncertain times in which we live.

Lisa Moses
Jerry Aldridge
Anarella Cellitti
Gwenyth McCorquodale

CHAPTER ONE
An Introduction and History of
Children's Fears Concerning War and Terrorism

Children in every corner of the planet are affected by war—or the threat of it.
They may experience war indirectly through television and the media, more
directly as they are forced to flee their country, or most directly, and tragically,
if they die as a result of armed conflict (Machel, 2003). The following information
tion is adapted from the fact sheet "The Impact of War on Children" (Machel,
2003):

- Armed conflict can result in civilian deaths as high as 90 percent of a given local population, with half of these victims being children.
- About 20 million children now live as refugees because they have had to leave their homes due to war, conflicts, or human rights violations.
- Over 6 million children have become disabled and 2 million have died because of war since 1990.
- Preventable infectious diseases and malnutrition have affected millions of refugees and children affected by war.
- Many children, both boys and girls, under the age of 18 have been forced to serve as soldiers, while others have joined armed conflicts to avoid poverty or to seek revenge for crimes committed against their families.
- Girls are often victims of violence, rape, prostitution, and mutilation during war.
- In war-torn areas, small firearms are easily obtained and used extensively in post-war conflict, resulting in the deaths of many children.
- In certain countries, such as Sierra Leone or Angola, almost one out of every three children dies before age 5. Armed conflict is a significant reason for this high rate of mortality.
- Great disparities exist in humanitarian relief efforts. Some countries affected by conflict receive substantial assistance, while others receive little or none. Children almost always suffer the most from such disparities.
- Finally, adults who want to assist not only children around the world but also their own children as they strive to cope with war often do not know how to help.

Although much research has been published on children's fears, relatively
little has been conducted on children's fears related to war and terrorism. This
chapter is divided into two main sections: the first section describes children's
fears in general and the second section focuses on children's specific fears
related to war and terrorism. The second section includes a brief, research-
based history of children's fears during war—beginning with World War II and
noting the effect of the Vietnam War, the Lebanese Civil War, the so-called Cold
War, and through to more recent concerns associated with the Gulf War, the
terrorist attacks of September 11, 2001, the ongoing anxiety of the Israeli-
Palestinian conflict, and the millions of refugee children around the world.

Children's Fears

To help children cope with fears in a time of war, a general understanding of what fear is and what children fear is valuable. Fears are quite common in children, and they are, in fact, normal developmental reactions that arise as responses to a perceived danger (Smith, Davidson, White, & Poppen, 1990). Most children's fears are about dangerous situations, physical harm, or animals. When children are fearful, they seek to defend themselves against perceived threats to their happiness or survival (Agne, 1996). While a certain amount of fear is necessary to normal development, unaddressed or excessive fear can lead to worries that deter development and impede growth, learning, and success (Crowley, 1981; Deluty & DeVitis, 1996). Fear is not the main problem; problems arise if a child is unable to cope with fear and the accompanying feelings of helplessness and despair (Giordano, 1987).

Parents and teachers are well aware of how a child's fears can affect the home and the classroom. One result is a disabling of learning. Fear curtails concentration and directs the child's focus toward the self, which diminishes motivation for the task at hand. Consequently, students experiencing fear suffer reduced levels of achievement (Agne, 1996).

Children in the 21st century are afraid of guns, death, and violence ("Age of Anxiety," 2001), and fear is not the only problem in an age of media violence. The American Academy of Pediatrics (2001) reviewed more than 3,500 studies concerning media violence and identified a variety of physical and mental health problems associated with exposure to violence through the media. These problems include depression, nightmares, and sleep disturbances. Clearly, the vivid discussions and depictions of violence and war found in the media pose a significant risk to children's health.

Many children also experience significant losses that can lead to fear. Recently, for example, thousands of children were affected when their parents, siblings, other relatives, or friends in the military were suddenly deployed to areas of conflict in the Middle East. In a remarkably short time, a loved one leaves and is gone for an indefinite period of time. In most cases, these children have received no preparation for the separation and the resulting feelings of loss.

Children are particularly vulnerable to loss because they are dependent on others. They cannot take care of themselves, and they know this. They have a developmental need for routine and security.

Children's limited understanding of the world also makes them incredibly vulnerable. While children are often aware of far more than their parents or teachers realize, they may be unable to cope with the information they take in, which can be devastating. Reality and fantasy often are blurred for young children, and their imaginations can bring them to irrational fears and illogical conclusions (Zimmer, 1987).

As children experience loss and fears, they may act out their feelings physically, although this is not always the case. Although children's ability to process loss improves as they acquire knowledge over time, they still experience shock and alarm, confusion, and strong emotions. If they are fortunate, they will experience some type of resolution as the loss is integrated and accepted (McGlauflin, 1992). Certain behaviors alert us to children's fears, including clinginess, dependency, and other problems, such as sleep disturbances, withdrawal, lessened attention and concentration, acting-out behaviors, and regression to behaviors typical of younger children.

While all children experience fears, children living in poverty are particularly subject to a wide range of fears (Garbarino, 1998). Often, socioeconomic status is itself a substantial stressor, especially when children live in poverty (Crawford, 1995). The impact of poverty on children's fears will be described in more detail in Chapter Two.

In general, we know that children cope with their fears better when the adults around them are supportive; when the environment is stable; when they receive consistent and loving care; when family relationships are stable; and when children feel a part of the family, school, and community. This is particularly true during times of war (McGlauflin, 1992).

Children's Fears Related to War and Terrorism

Children are especially afraid during times of war and threats of terrorism. The most common fears children experience during these times are fears about separation, abandonment, physical danger or injury, and death. Children who already have experienced losses are often the most vulnerable, and so they may have stronger reactions to war or threats of terrorism (Zimmer, 1987, 1992). During a time of war, children's assumptions are shattered. They no longer believe that they or their families are safe. Their primary concern is their own safety and the safety of those who care for them (Zimmer, 1992). While children's understanding of war may be minimal, their fantasies can run wild. Children's images of war may include bombs being dropped on their homes, for example, even if their country is unlikely to experience bombing. For some children, such worries may seem unreasonable; yet to them, they are quite possible (Waddell & Thomas, 1992). And many children throughout the world face a very real possibility of loss, suffering, and even death as a result of war.

Research on children in war zones documents some immediate responses to war. Byrnes (2001) found that children develop characteristics of fear and anxiety, which may include aggressive play, acting tough to hide fears, and dulled senses manifested as an inability to care for and respond emotionally to others. Many children of war experience night terrors, nightmares, and other sleep disturbances such as bed-wetting (Allan & Anderson, 1986). Thus, it is not surprising that children of war experience learning problems (Byrnes, 2001). Routines become nonexistent, schooling and health care are disrupted, and children may even experience or witness such devastating catastrophes as burned houses and destroyed communities. In these situations, children are torn from all that is familiar to them. Such disruptions affect the quality of children's lives long after the violence is over (Allan & Anderson, 1986).

For many, the results of war include the loss of childhood. As families experience war-related losses and separations, many young children take on the responsibility of caring for younger siblings. Play and innocence are put aside. Although children in war zones leave childhood behind in one sense, they experience restricted development in another. During times of war, children miss many opportunities to learn, play, grow, and just be children.

Children of war see and experience real violence—not just the threat of violence or images on television. Children in some countries even may become aggressors themselves, as they are enlisted into the military. The moral development of these children is severely altered as a result of this direct involvement in war. Both violence and fear of violence are debilitating to development (Byrnes, 2001).

While it is impossible to report on all of the world conflicts in which children have been involved or are now experiencing, the numerous studies about children's fears related to war and terrorism that have been conducted from World War II to the present are enlightening. Here, we take a look at children's fears during World War II, the Vietnam War, the Lebanese Civil War, the Cold War, the Gulf War, the terrorist attacks of September 11, 2001, and the current Israeli-Palestinian conflict. We also reflect on the experiences of millions of war-created refugee children on the African continent and elsewhere.

World War II
During and shortly after World War II, several studies of children's fears were conducted. Gardner (1943) surveyed 49 young children to ascertain their behaviors during the year following the attack on Pearl Harbor. In the families of the children studied, 15 fathers and 43 brothers had entered military service. Gardner found that only 12 children exhibited fear, anxiety, and grief as immediate reactions to their loved ones' enlistment, and that such feelings, with the exception of a single case, were transient. He concluded that most children in this study withstood the test of separation from a family member quite well.

Rautman and Brower (1945) found that children often reflect the interests, activities, and worries of the adults who are important in their lives. From this perspective, they investigated the extent to which elementary school children were preoccupied with war and war-related activities. Children as a whole did not appear to be unduly preoccupied with war or war activities. However, the researchers did identify a trend for higher preoccupation with war as a child's age increased.

Bender and Frosch (1942) sought to answer the following four important questions in their study: 1) What were the attitudes of children concerning war? 2) What effect, if any, did the war have on children's thinking, feeling, and behavior? 3) Were there any differences in the effect of war on normal children as compared to children who were suffering from a determined psychological disorder? 4) What types of children were most influenced by war? Bender and Frosch found that children were influenced by the way their parents, their older siblings, their school teachers, and their playmates coped with the anxieties created by the war. Generally, anxiety arose when the war threatened the family structure. More difficulties were found with children whose home lives and relationships with parents or guardians were under the constant threat of change.

Researchers in this era also investigated children's thinking during wartime and peacetime (Rautman & Brower, 1945). By early 1950, children were clearly less preoccupied with war and related themes than during World War II; nevertheless, some children were still concerned about the death of a loved one or were fearful that someone they know would be killed. War as a factor in children's thinking seems to vary with the times. However, children's concerns about death and killing by one means or another appear to be constant features of even young children's lives.

The Vietnam War
Several studies have examined the effects of the Vietnam War on Vietnamese children (Church & Angelo, 1995; Goldson, 1996; Savitz, Thang, Swenson, & Stone, 1993; Williams, 1997; Zhou & Bankston, 2000). One group of children affected by the Vietnam War, those born in Vietnam and raised in the United

States, was of particular interest. These children endured the trials and difficulties of living as refugees. Most spent time in a refugee camp prior to their entry into the United States, and many were separated from their families during this time. Poverty and cultural differences presented special challenges to them. Despite these adversities, many displayed impressive resiliency and developed a reputation for outstanding academic achievement. The social processes of many Vietnamese families were contributing factors in helping these children overcome many of the difficult issues they faced (Zhou & Bankston, 2000).

Other studies focused on U.S. children and the Vietnam War (Alvik, 1968; Key, 1964; Lipset, 1996; Tolley, 1973). Many children living in the United States during the Vietnam War held serious misconceptions about the war. Children from lower income families tended to be more accepting of the war, while children from higher income families tended to know more facts about the war (Tolley, 1973). While children had varying levels of acceptance and misconceptions about the war, this was one of the first wars to bombard children's senses on a daily basis through television. Media images of war were a common, sometimes even daily, part of many children's experiences during this time.

Young children who lived in Cambodia under the Khmer Rouge during the war also were the subjects of study, and researchers found that, four years after the conflict ended, 50 percent of the children still manifested symptoms of posttraumatic stress disorder (PTSD). PTSD is characterized by emotional numbing, intrusive ideas and feelings, and diminished expectations for the future, among other symptoms (Byrnes, 2001).

The Lebanese Civil War
Der-Karabetian (1984) explored the coping strategies of Lebanese American children who experienced the Lebanese civil war of 1975-1977. The study involved 46 males and 41 females. Fifty-two of these children had been directly exposed to shelling, and 35 had not been exposed to shelling. Although the group exposed to the shelling did show several differences concerning the presence of stress symptoms, they did not evidence any severe pathology. Der-Karabetian theorized that children gradually become less sensitive to daily threats. He attributed the children's general good health to the incorporation of mutual support into effective protective strategies that were part of daily life, noting that caring adults provided much support, as well. Honig (1986), however, reported a different view of these children. She suggested that children's nervousness, nightmares, and sleep disturbances necessitated active intervention by child psychologists.

The Cold War
In the mid to late 20th century, during the Cold War, many children around the world feared a nuclear strike. During this time, children were getting most of their information about nuclear weapons from either television or school. According to Beardslee and Mack (1986), about 40 percent of children between 5 and 12 were concerned about nuclear threat. Children from New Zealand, the United States, and the Soviet Union all expressed fears of nuclear war. Whereas only 58.2 percent of American children were worried about nuclear war, 98.6 percent of Soviet children were concerned (Chivian, Mack, & Waletzky, 1983). Older children had more fears, as their capacity to understand the

nature of nuclear war was greater. Phillips (1985), however, found contradictory indications that younger children were more fearful than adolescents with regard to nuclear incidents. She explained that while conventional bombs convey very concrete images, including charred ruins and corpses, for older children, the threats of radiation were too abstract and intangible to fully understand. Phillips cautioned that adults should not conclude that preschool and primary school children were less afraid of nuclear war because they were less informed or less cognitively capable of understanding it.

A major fear that children experienced concerning nuclear war had to do with their fears about their families. Children feared dying less than being left without support and care. They often did not discuss such fears openly with family members; parents or guardians often were unaware that their children were harboring these fears (Phillips, 1985).

The Gulf War
In November of 1991, more than 110,000 students responded to surveys about the first Gulf War. Published in nine various *Scholastic* magazines, the results indicated that the Gulf War was having a large impact on children's lives. Forty percent of the students surveyed in the United States said they knew of someone who was a soldier and had been sent to the Middle East, and 13 percent indicated that a family member was there. More than half of the students said they were scared, while approximately one third felt angry. Well over 50 percent worried about war, and nearly a third worried a family member or someone they knew would have to fight. Many children's fears became a reality. Of course, children in both the United States and the Middle East lost parents during the Gulf War (Stern, 2001).

While the Gulf War received a considerable amount of media attention, for many children the images of war lacked reality and even took on a video game-like quality. The images from press conferences and briefings focused on precision bombings and included no U.S. American casualties. Thus, most of the children in the United States did not receive a realistic picture of war (Kazemek, 1999).

A real concern of many adults during the Gulf War was providing emotional support for those children with family members stationed in the Gulf. The assignment away from home of a single parent, both parents, or the mother resulted in over 17,000 children being left with friends or relatives. Many of these children struggled to cope with a fear of abandonment (Hostetler, 1991).

Children's Fears Following September 11, 2001
The dramatic events of September 11, 2001, demanded another look at children's fears related to war and terrorism. More lives were lost on that day than during the attack on Pearl Harbor (Sullivan, 2002). Around the United States, teachers were confronting, with children, the images of what had happened, which were played again and again on television. They struggled to shield the children from such images or to help them make sense of them. Due to recent incidents involving school shootings in several U.S. communities, schools had developed crisis management plans for school safety. The terrorist attacks, however, posed a huge challenge—how to ease children's worries about a world outside that suddenly seemed vastly different and unpredictable (Newcomb, 2001). While adults struggled to cope with the devastating nature of these events and their implications, children were even less prepared (Cook, 2001).

Children Directly Exposed to the Attacks.

A 10-year-old boy is afraid to go back to his school—ever. A 7-year-old girl wants to know whether the World Trade Center will be rebuilt, and insists that it was empty and that no one was hurt, despite her parents' gentle attempts to tell her the truth. A boy at Stuyvesant High School watched from a window of the school library as people fell or jumped to their deaths from the burning twin towers a few blocks south. A classmate standing next to him crossed himself every time a body catapulted into empty air. And the [first] boy, who is Jewish, wished that he could do something, if only to make such symbolic gestures himself. They were among hundreds of schoolchildren in Lower Manhattan who witnessed the attack on the World Trade Center. Some were still lining up in playgrounds to go into classes as the first plane slammed into the north tower, others had front-row views from the windows of their classrooms; a few were still walking to school holding their parents' hands as the horrific scene unfolded in the sky before them. (Hartocollis, 2001, p. A2).

Children who saw the events of September 11 may act out the violence and might try, through their play, to "magically" change the outcome. They may show more anger or exhibit other behaviors. Younger children may show other signs of stress, including an increased fear of noises and the dark, difficulty concentrating, difficulty sleeping and loss of appetite, a return to bed-wetting, and temper tantrums. Feelings of shock, disbelief, anger, and grief are some symptoms of traumatic stress. These are the reactions of children who face a tragedy of such proportions as the events of September 11th. Some may experience physical problems, such as stomachaches, headaches, rashes, and cold- and flu-like symptoms (American National Red Cross, 2001b).

The American National Red Cross addressed some of the fears and feelings of children who were directly exposed to the attacks. Some of these fears included fear for their personal safety, fear for the safety of their loved ones, and fear for the safety of the country (American National Red Cross, 2001a).

When children's preoccupation with traumatic events retains intensity three weeks after the disaster, they may need professional help. Professional help also may be recommended if children are still experiencing changes such as sleep disturbances, angry outbursts, or depression three months after the trauma (American National Red Cross, 2001a). The prevalence of serious stress disorders among children affected by the terrorist attacks might not be known for some time (Hartocollis, 2001).

As the war on terrorism unfolds, children who have parents in the military may face additional fears. Some children are at particular risk; in 120,000 U.S. families, both parents are in the military. This creates a relatively new situation in that many children are temporarily in need of being raised by someone other than their parents. Because one of the major fears that young children experience is the fear of abandonment, this situation could have a profound influence on their development (Stern, 2001).

Children Not Directly Exposed to the Attacks.
Many children throughout the world were affected by the attacks of September 11, 2001, even if not directly so. They were exposed to the events of September 11th again and

again through television broadcasts. In dealing with traumatic events such as this, teachers and parents must keep in mind that the news media, particularly television, do not consider the developmental levels and needs of young children. For this reason, the daily news usually is not appropriate for young children. Protecting children from watching the news, however, will not necessarily prevent them from hearing about traumatic events. Parents, educators, and concerned adults should be prepared to address children's feelings and needs during threats of war and terrorism (Ucci, 2001).

Felton and Hausman (2002) expressed concern that so much of what children are experiencing comes through television, radio, and computers. Children receive an overload of information and repetitive hype. It is easy for them to become mesmerized and transfixed by this onslaught. As caring adults, parents and teachers must be aware of children's vulnerability in order to properly protect them.

Following a disaster, most people are eager to hear the latest news about what happened. Disaster research shows, however, that unexpected stories or images on television about a disaster often cause a recurrence of stress-related problems in children (American National Red Cross, 2001a). The American National Red Cross strongly recommends that children not be allowed to watch news coverage of a disaster. Adults who view and review the damage also are at risk of becoming secondary victims; they are more likely to suffer emotional and physical problems.

Even if not directly affected by the events of September 11, 2001, most children are confused to some extent about what happened and about their feelings connected with the attacks. Some children may appear unaffected by what they saw and heard. Not everyone has an immediate reaction to such events; some may have delayed reactions that show up days, weeks, or even months later, and some may never react. A number of common reactions and problems were observed in children following the September 11th disaster. Some children displayed feelings of shame, sadness, anger, fear, and/or guilt; some experienced trouble falling asleep or staying asleep, nightmares, changes in appetite, problems in school, and/or feelings of helplessness; and some sought additional solitude, and/or were moody and irritable (American National Red Cross, 2001b).

When their safety is threatened, children feel insecure and fearful. These children need frequent reassurance that they will be cared for and will not be abandoned. Remember, fear of abandonment is a major childhood fear; during war, it has an especially strong hold on many children. Young children cannot clearly understand the concept of permanent loss. As children reach school age, however, they begin to understand the permanence of loss from a trauma. They can become preoccupied with loss, or potential loss, and may want to talk about it continually; or, they may repeatedly role-play a traumatic event. They may have trouble concentrating in school. Because their thinking is more mature, their understanding of a disaster like September 11th is more complete. Such feelings and reactions should generally disappear within 4 to 6 weeks, as children resume their daily activities and focus their attention on other things (American National Red Cross, 2001c).

The Israeli-Palestinian Conflict
Certain areas of the world have been subject to years of war and conflict. In Israel, many children experience nervousness, nightmares, and other sleep

difficulties that necessitate the active intervention of child psychologists (Honig, 1986). Children who receive such intervention are fortunate; the vast majority of children affected by war and terrorism receive no such services.

Studies have been conducted in Israel concerning the effects of war, terrorism, and violence on children (Fields-Meyer & Norman, 2002). Fields-Meyer and Norman (2002) conducted a case study with two families; one family was Palestinian and the other Israeli. These two families were separated by just one mile, and each family suffered from the death of a child due to the ongoing conflict. The Israeli family's 27-year-old daughter was killed during a suicide bombing as she sat with friends in a café in downtown Jerusalem. The Palestinian family lost their 19-year-old son to a sniper's bullet as he went to an upstairs room to retrieve a blanket for his 6-year-old brother. The young child witnessed his older brother's death, but cannot understand why his brother is not coming home. Both families live in fear and are constantly aware that even everyday routines, such as going to the grocery store, carry a risk.

Children Who Are Refugees Because of War
Throughout the continent of Africa, approximately 3 million people are refugees from political persecution, famine, and tribal hostilities. Children are more vulnerable, both physically and emotionally, to the hardships of refugee life than adults. Many refugee children must confront multiple traumas, including the death of parents, grandparents, and siblings. The children witness war firsthand, often observing the destruction of their homes and communities and the loss of friends. Hunger and violence are constants, as is a sense of powerlessness. Previous sources of security and sustenance are gone (Benjamin & Morgan, 1989).

Approximately 12 million refugees seek shelter around the world. Crises in Afghanistan, Iran, Iraq, Vietnam, Laos, Cambodia, and Cuba all have led to refugee activity. Many refugee children experience physical problems caused by inadequate nutrition, lack of concentration due to chronic stress, and injuries suffered before or during flight. Many have emotional problems as they become alienated from their countries and communities, suffer anxiety as they perceive their guardians' powerlessness to protect them from the many hardships of the refugee experience, and experience disorientation and loss of identity (Benjamin & Morgan, 1989).

Conclusion
There is no doubt that fears of war and terrorism influence a large majority of children on this planet. How do we help children cope with these fears? Three important factors must be considered: 1) the child's context and personal circumstances, 2) the child's temperament, and 3) the child's age. Chapter Two addresses context and culture as powerful influences on how a child deals with fears related to war. Chapter Three focuses on the child's temperament and personality, and how some children cope by turning inward, while others externalize and act out their hostility and aggression. Chapter Four examines how age makes a difference in a child's fears and how adults can help. Chapter Five demonstrates how literature and storytelling can be important tools with which to address children's fears, while Chapter Six discusses the use of aesthetics to make a difference. Throughout the book, we have provided references and resources for further information about helping every child deal with fears, especially those related to war and terrorism.

References

Age of Anxiety, The. (2001, June 10). *New York Times Magazine*, pp. 36-37.

Agne, K. (1996). Fear: The teacher's teacher. *Educational Horizons, 74*, 130-133.

Allan, J., & Anderson, E. (1986). Children and crises: A developmental guidance approach. *Elementary School Guidance and Counseling, 21*, 143-149.

Alvik, T. (1968). The development of views on conflict, war and peace among school children. *Journal of Peace Research, 5*, 171-195.

American Academy of Pediatrics, Committee on Public Education. (2001). Media violence. *Pediatrics, 108*, 1222-1226.

American National Red Cross. (2001a). *Helping young children cope with trauma* [Brochure]. Baltimore: Author.

American National Red Cross. (2001b). *When bad things happen* [Brochure]. Baltimore: Author.

American National Red Cross. (2001c). *Why do I feel like this?* [Brochure]. Baltimore: Author.

Beardslee, W. R., & Mack, J. E. (1986). Youth and children and the nuclear threat. *Newsletter of the Society for Research in Child Development, Inc.*, 1-2.

Bender, L., & Frosch, J. (1942, October). *Children's reactions to the war.* Paper presented to the New York Society for Child Psychiatry, New York.

Benjamin, M., & Morgan, P. (1989). *Refugee children traumatized by war and violence: The challenge offered to the service delivery system.* (ERIC Document Reproduction Service No. ED 326598).

Byrnes, D. (2001). War and conflict: Educators advocating for the protection of children. *Educational Forum, 65*, 227-232.

Chivian, E., Mack, J., & Waletzky, J. (1983, August). *What Soviet children are saying about nuclear war: Project summary.* Paper presented at the meeting of the Nuclear Psychology Program, Harvard Medical School, New York.

Church, G., & Angelo, B. (1995, April 24). The final 10 days. *Time, 145*, 24-34.

Cook, W. (2001). *Stress: Helping kids through crisis situations.* Retrieved October 26, 2002, from www.mayoclinic.com/invoke.cfm?id=FL00072

Crawford, S. (1995). Intensity and frequency of children's fears: Gender differences, ethnicity, income level (Doctoral dissertation, University of North Carolina, 1995). *Dissertation Abstracts International, 56*, 06A.

Crowley, J. (1981). Worries of elementary school students. *Elementary School Guidance and Counseling, 16*, 98-102.

Deluty, R., & DeVitis, J. (1996). Fears in the classroom: Psychological issues and pedagogical implications. *Educational Horizons, 74*, 108-113.

Der-Karabetian, A. (1984). *Reaction of Armenian children to wartime stress in Lebanon.* Los Angeles, CA: Counseling and Personnel Services. (ERIC Document Reproduction Service No. ED 251732)

Felton, R., & Hausman, J. (2002). Transcending tragedy: Global communication draws us together. *Arts & Activities, 5*, 24-27.

Fields-Meyer, T., & Norman, P. (2002, April 29). World apart. *People, 57*, 52-57.

Garbarino, J. (1998). *Children in danger: Coping with the consequences of community violence.* San Francisco: Jossey-Bass.

Gardner, F. (1943, April). *Mental hygiene.* Paper presented at the National Conference of the American Association of Psychiatric Social Workers, New York.

Giordano, G. (1987). Rechanneling anxieties. *Academic Therapy, 22*, 535-538.

Goldson, E. (1996). The effect of war on children. *Child Abuse & Neglect: The International Journal, 20*, 809-819.

Hartocollis, A. (2001, September 13). As witnesses to tragedy, students confront fears. *New York Times*, p. A2.

Honig, A. (1986). Stress and coping in children. *Young Children, 41*(4), 50-63.

Hostetler, L. (1991). From our president. Scuds, sorties, and yellow ribbons: The costs of war for children. *Young Children, 46*, 2.

Kazemek, F. (1999). Intelligent people seek peace: Exploring the Vietnam War with middle school students. *Middle School Journal, 31*, 18-24.

Key, V. (1964). *Public opinion and American democracy.* New York: Alfred A. Knopf.

Lipset, S. (1996). *Political man.* Garden City, NY: Doubleday.

Machel, G. (2003). *The impact of war on children: Fact sheet.* Retrieved March 1, 2003, from www.unicef.org/children-in-war/machel/fact.htm

McGlauflin, H. (1992). How children grieve: Implications for counseling. In G. R. Walz & J. C. Bleuer (Eds.), *Developing support groups for students: Helping students cope with crisis* (pp. 11-20). Ann Arbor, MI: ERIC Clearinghouse on Counseling and Personnel Services.

Newcomb, A. (2001). Where's the lesson plan for this? *Christian Science Monitor, 93*, 15.

Phillips, S. (1985). *Children's and youth's anxiety about nuclear threat.* San Francisco: North Shore Hospital. (ERIC Document Reproduction Service ED 270201).

Rautman, A., & Brower, E. (1945). War themes in children's stories. *Journal of Psychology, 19*, 191-202.

Savitz, D., Thang, N., Swenson, I., & Stone, E. (1993). Vietnamese infant and childhood mortality in relation to the Vietnam War. *American Journal of Public Health, 83*, 1134-1138.

Smith, D., Davidson, P., White, P., & Poppen, W. (1990). An integrative theoretical model of children's fears. *Home Economics Research Journal, 19*, 151-158.

Stern, S. (2001). New worry: Kids with both parents in combat. *Christian Science Monitor, 93*, 1.

Sullivan, R. (Ed.). (2002). *One nation: America remembers September 11, 2001.* New York: Little, Brown & Co.

Tolley, H. (1973). *Children and war: Political socialization to international conflict.* New York: Teachers College Press.

Ucci, M. (2001). Helping children cope with personal and public tragedies. *Child Health Alert, 9*, 4-6.

Waddell, D., & Thomas, A. (1992). Children and war—Responding to Operation Desert Storm. In G. R. Walz & J. C. Bleuer (Eds.), *Developing support groups for students: Helping students cope with crisis* (pp. 61-63). Ann Arbor, MI: ERIC Clearinghouse on Counseling and Personnel Services.

Williams, G. (1997). I could always hear the screams of the children. *Biography, 9*, 32-38.

Zhou, M., & Bankston, C. (2000). *The experience of Vietnamese refugee children in the United States.* (Report No. ED-99-CO-0035). New York: ERIC Clearinghouse on Urban Education.

Zimmer, E. (1987). Responding to suicide in schools: A case in loss interventions and group survivorship. *Journal of Counseling and Development, 65*, 499-501.

Zimmer, J. (1992). Helping children cope with war. In G. R. Walz & J. C. Bleuer (Eds.), *Developing support groups for students: Helping students cope with crisis* (pp. 21-23). Ann Arbor, MI: ERIC Clearinghouse on Counseling and Personnel Services.

CHAPTER TWO
The Impact of Context
on Children's Fears

Russell is an only child who lives in Stamford, Connecticut, with his parents. His family would be considered upper-middle class. Russell's mom stays home and takes the responsibility of home schooling him. His parents limit his television viewing and shelter him from all news programs. His parents have worked hard to protect Russell from hearing about war or terrorism. As a result, Russell has little concern about armed conflicts or the threat of terrorism.

Javier is a homeless child living on the streets of Mexico City. He squats with a group of children near the Zona Rosa, where they beg for money and food. Javier has seen crime and violence all of his life. Recently, he found another child on the sidewalk, dead. Javier, like Russell, does not watch television. He knows nothing of armed conflicts around the world or threats of international terrorism. Nevertheless, he lives in fear because he experiences "street wars" and violence on a daily basis.

Nichole lives in the small town of Eutaw, Alabama, with her mother. Nichole and her mother have few family members in their area. They do not know anyone serving in the military. While Nichole occasionally hears about the threat of war and terrorism on television, she is not worried. When Nichole has questions about what she hears, she discusses them with her mom. Her mom reassures her that "everything is OK and the family is safe and secure."

Meredith lives about one hour's drive from Nichole in Thomasville, Alabama. Meredith's situation is similar in many ways to Nichole's. They both live in small, Southern, rural towns. Meredith lives with both parents, but recently her world was turned upside down. Over 1,600 military personnel in her small community were sent overseas into conflict zones. Meredith's mom, dad, an uncle, and a cousin left home abruptly for military service. Meredith was sent to live with her aging grandparents in a neighboring town. She has transferred to another school where she knows no one. She worries about her parents and her extended family who have gone away to serve their country.

Foday was just a young child living near Freetown, Sierra Leone, when he was kidnapped by the Revolutionary United Front (RUF). Since the mid-1990s, he has grown up in a child army that has terrorized the country. As a member of the RUF, he has killed and mutilated other children, cutting off their arms and legs with machetes.

Kabanda's parents were killed by soldiers when he was just 9 years old. His family lived in the path of the RUF's destruction. It is quite possible that Foday, or a child in similar circumstances, killed Kabanda's parents. Kabanda says, "The men who killed my mother, they make me angry. Me, I decide to go into the army. Me, I decide to beat them. If I find them, I kill them." ("Children and War," 1994, p. 6)

These vignettes highlight how context can affect children's fears during a time of war or terrorism. Children in different contexts confront vastly different challenges. While it would be impossible to report on all of the possible contexts in which children live, three contexts are important to our understanding of children's fears concerning war and terrorism: 1) children with family members who have been quickly deployed to areas of conflict for military duty, 2) children of poverty, and 3) children who live in the midst of armed conflicts.

Children With Family Members Who Have Been Quickly Deployed for Military Duty

When children have family or friends in the military, the possibility of separation is always present. In some cases, families have months to prepare for the separation. In other cases, loved ones are deployed very quickly for service. During the preparations for war with Iraq, many U.S. military personnel were sent overseas with very little notice. In these circumstances, the children of military families are affected immediately and need support and guidance.

The American School Counselor Association (ASCA) offers information related to deployment issues on its Web site (ASCA, 2003). They report that children separated from family due to military service commonly react with fear and anger; they feel a loss of control and a loss of stability. ASCA explains that children and adults can progress through stages of separation, beginning with the anticipation of separation, moving into detachment just prior to the separation, and, finally, experiencing emotional disorganization for approximately one to two months after the adult is gone.

Suggestions for Caregivers (Parents or Guardians) Left Behind
- If at all possible, prepare the child in advance for a family member's deployment. When family members have to leave quickly, it is important to support the child during this short and difficult time.
- If possible, help the deployed family member to make a video for the child to watch as often as he or she would like. The video should be upbeat and designed to comfort the child while the family member is away.
- Remember that you serve as a role model for the child who feels abandoned. Children will pick up on your fears and anxiety, so "don't project your fears onto your children" (ASCA, 2003, p. 3).
- Be truthful about the event. Explain that the deployed family member had to go quickly, and emphasize that it was not the child's fault. The child did not cause the parent to leave.
- "Help children communicate with the loved one who is away—letters, E-mails, pictures" (ASCA, 2003, p. 3).
- Maintain routines as much as possible. If a child must change place of residence or school while a guardian is away, provide continuity and establish stable routines as quickly as possible. All children need predictable structure, and this is especially true for those who have a loved one who was called away quickly for military duty.
- Talk with school counselors and teachers, and ask them to assist in helping the child.
- Talk with the child often and listen carefully to what the child has to say. Lines of communication should be continually open.
- When necessary, seek professional help for yourself and the child.

Children of Poverty

Children from low-income homes experience more frequent and intense fears than do children from middle-class homes (Coeyman, 2001; Crawford, 1995; Honig, 1986; Miller, 1997; Schmitz, 1992). Children of poverty often live in circumstances that promote fear and insecurity. This sense of insecurity influences academic performance, social competence, emotional development, and coping strategies, especially when survival is the primary focus in a child's life (Coeyman, 2001).

Children from lower socioeconomic homes tend to be more fearful of gangs, and of violence in general. Exposure to crime, which is more prevalent in lower socioeconomic neighborhoods, not only encourages children's fears but often distorts their understanding of death (Miller, 1997). Miller found that African American children living in poverty showed a 27 percent higher level of anxiety about death than more economically comfortable European American children. He also found that 97 percent of children in his study had a desire to talk with adults about death and violence, but did not do so because they feared upsetting their parents or teachers.

Children of poverty who witness family violence are more likely to be aggressive and to develop other forms of antisocial behavior; they also may connect these events to terrorist attacks (Coeyman, 2001). The interaction of crime, violence, and fear diminishes the emotional health of many children from low-income homes. For children who live in a constant state of fear, traumatic events can reactivate emotions associated with previous traumas (American National Red Cross, 2001).

Children of poverty are more likely to fear war or terrorism than are children from middle-class homes. Moses (2002) interviewed kindergarten children from both middle-class and lower socioeconomic homes to determine their perceptions, misunderstandings, and fears concerning the "War on Terrorism" in the United States after September 11, 2001. No child from the middle socioeconomic group in her study expressed any fears related to terrorism. However, the majority of children from the low-income group expressed multiple fears related to terrorism, including: 1) fears related to being hurt, someone loved being hurt, or property damage; 2) fears related to "bad" people coming into the home; 3) fears about having to fight bad people; 4) fears of scary things related to war; and 5) fears of bad dreams.

Fears Related to Being Hurt, Someone Loved Being Hurt, or Property Damage. The threat of physical harm to the child, to someone the child loves, or to property weighed heavily on the minds of the children in Moses's 2002 study. This was the most common fear of children from low socioeconomic homes. They expressed numerous fears about being hurt in some way. The children made comments such as, "They have guns and stuff to hurt me," "They can kill me with a gun," and "They want to kill me." One child thought the terrorists wanted to make him their slave, tie him up, and cut off his fingers. One child said she thought about being hurt day and night, and that she was afraid they might set her house on fire while she and her family were inside. Another child also reported believing the terrorists would try to get him at his house. This same child was afraid that someone was trying to kill his "pawpaw" [grandfather], even though his grandfather had a secret hiding place. Fears about the windows exploding, the house being knocked down while they were there, and the door getting shot down were also reported by the children.

Fears Related to Bad People Coming to the Home. The second biggest fear of the kindergarten children in Moses's (2002) study was that of bad guys coming to their home. One child thought mean army guys kept coming to his house. He said he had built a scarecrow to keep the "sneakers" away from the basement. Several of the children believed that the mean army guys were going to steal from their families, and do great physical damage to their homes. One child said that he knew bad people were in his neighborhood, because he had witnessed a fight at his house between four people who were trying to kill each other with knives. He believed that these individuals, as well as other bad people, were "from the war."

Fears Related to Having To Fight Bad People. Children from poor homes also expressed the fear that they would have to actually become physically involved in a fight with the bad guys. Each child who expressed this fear also seemed to be confident in his or her ability to successfully defeat the aggressor. They reported that they could shoot a gun if they had to, could fight really fast, and could hit hard. One of the children indicated he would be fighting them with knives, that he would choke their heads off, and that he could hit them once and they would be dead. Another child reported she would knock them down with her feet, and still another child spoke of having assistance with the fight from his robot. One child pledged that when the mean army guys came to his basement, he would defeat them once he put on his Ninja suit.

Fears of Scary Things Related to War. Children from low-income homes expressed fears of scary things that reflected their understanding of war. One child spoke of seeing some monsters in a cave in his basement. He then clarified his statement by saying, "The monsters really were 'sneakers,' the mean army people." Another child explained in some detail how she had seen a man with a mask outside her brother's window at night. She said that the person wearing the mask was actually "London" (Osama Bin Laden), but he reminded her of "Scream" (the name she gave to a scary character in a horror movie). Still another child expressed some of his nighttime fears when he said, "bad people, monster people, are trying to kill me."

Fears of Bad Dreams. Each child who expressed fears spoke of having bad dreams about those fears. The bad dreams were generally about people dying, bad people trying to kill the child or his relatives, or some bad person knocking down the child's home. The child who expressed her dreams about her house being knocked down also said she had dreams in which her house was knocked down and set on fire, killing her and her whole family. "I dreamed they killed us all [her family]," she said sadly. The children reported being afraid of their bad dreams. One child said that, since the attacks, she had been allowed to sleep with her little brother because she was afraid to sleep by herself. Another child was determined not to have bad dreams. "No way!" he said. "I wouldn't dream about those guys!" (Moses, 2002, p. 144).

Ways To Help Children of Poverty Cope With Their
Fears Related to War and Terrorism

- Make sure that children are aware that caring adults are available to talk with and listen to them about their concerns. Be specific about who these adults are and how the children can find them.
- Make efforts to recruit mentors.
- Provide training concerning children's fears to mentors already working with children of poverty, as well as to newly recruited mentors.
- Consistently present the school as a safe and caring place for the children. Casually incorporate examples of school security and caring when talking with the children. Help raise the children's awareness of how many individuals are working to keep them safe, and identify them all.
- Make any effort necessary to relieve any known personal or environmental stressors, such as hunger or lack of appropriate shelter, that the children are experiencing. The more personal and emotional stressors a child experiences, the more difficulties and psychological discomforts he will experience during a traumatic time.
- Give the children clear, concise, and accurate facts concerning a traumatic event. Keep in mind children's developmental levels, and provide only that information needed to satisfy their current questions or alter their perceived misunderstandings. Never lie to children. Use words or phrases that won't confuse them. Work hard to make sure they understand your intended meaning.
- Listen to children and watch for evidence of misunderstandings and fears. Address these in a direct, caring, and empathic manner. Help children distinguish between fantasy and reality.
- Reassure children that attempts are being made to ensure an adult will always be available during school to care for them.
- Watch for behavioral demonstrations or psychosomatic reactions (such as headaches or digestive problems). These may be cues that certain children have unmet needs concerning their fears.
- Keep children's physical environment as calm and orderly as possible. The physical environment can dramatically influence children's reactions and affect manifestations of difficulties.
- Build children's self-confidence by involving them in as many problem-solving situations as possible. This helps create a sense of empowerment and control that can help children feel more secure.

- Allow children to make as many choices as possible to help alleviate any feelings of helplessness or loss of control. Although these choices may be about trivial matters, the process of making choices will boost children's self-esteem. Having choices strengthens children's belief that they have some control over their lives, which often helps them cope more effectively with external stressors.
- Be patient with children and take seriously their reactions to a traumatic event. Be aware that, because they may have experienced other traumas in the past, children from low-income environments may have a more difficult time dealing with events that typically trigger fears in children.
- Accept the various ways children express their feelings and reactions. Some children may become withdrawn and be unwilling to talk about an event, while others may become intensely sad or angry. When these feelings or reactions become destructive to the self or others, seek the appropriate referrals for help and guidance.
- Encourage and support the parents and caregivers of children in poverty. Information and support can be made available to parents through media presentations, group meetings, written materials, or informal conferences.
- Allow children of poverty to be more dependent on you for a period of time after a traumatic event. After support, care, and counseling are provided, children often will begin to develop renewed independence.

Children Who Live in the Midst of Armed Conflicts

One of the most difficult contexts for children is direct involvement in a war. Some children see their parents and family members killed before their eyes, some children are wounded themselves, others become refugees, and some children take part in war as soldiers. To address these dangers to children, the United Nations has developed a 78-page document called "The Impact of Armed Conflict on Children" (1996), and the International Convention on the Rights of Children has published "Children and War" (1994).

Children suffer in many ways when they live in the midst of war. Rationing, sanctions, disease, landmines, and the psychological impact of war have a long-range, devastating influence ("Children and War," 1994). Children in all parts of the world experience war. Children in certain Latin American countries suffer because of extreme poverty and gang wars. Children in some parts of Europe are temporarily or permanently separated from their parents because of armed conflicts. Many children in the Middle East grow up without knowing anything other than war, and children throughout Asia are killed or maimed because of landmines left over from past wars. Furthermore, many of these conflicts take place in areas of the world where it is difficult to meet children's basic needs, even during times of peace ("Children and War," 1994).

When children are used as soldiers, their lives are in continual danger. As "The Impact of Armed Conflict on Children" (1996) reports:

Once recruited as soldiers, children generally receive much the same treatment as adults—including the often brutal induction ceremonies. Many start out in support functions which entail great risk and hardship. One of the common tasks assigned to children is to serve as porters, often carrying very heavy loads of up to 60 kilograms including ammunition or injured soldiers. Children who are too weak to carry their loads are liable to be savagely beaten or even shot. Children are also used for household and other routine duties. In Uganda, child soldiers have often done guard duty, worked in the gardens, hunted for wild fruits and vegetables and looted food from gardens and granaries. Children have also been used extensively in many countries as lookouts and messengers. While this last role may seem less life-threatening than others, in fact it puts all children under suspicion. In Latin America, reports tell of government forces that have deliberately killed even the youngest children in peasant communities on the grounds that they, too, were dangerous. . . . Although the majority of child soldiers are boys, armed groups also recruit girls, many of whom perform the same functions as boys. (p. 13)

Suggestions for Adults To Help Children Who Serve As Soldiers
"The Impact of Armed Conflict on Children" (1996) provides specific ways for individuals, organizations, and governments to assist children who serve as soldiers. Clearly, this is a macrosystems issue, requiring more than individual or small-group efforts to correct this injustice. "The Impact of Armed Conflict on Children" (1996) provides a blueprint for what governments can do to ensure that children do not serve as soldiers. Two suggestions for organizations and governments covered in significant detail in this document are:

- *Work for demobilization and reintegration into society.* "Reintegration programmes must re-establish contact with the family and the community. . . . In many cases, reunification is impossible. . . . Effective social reintegration depends upon support from . . . communities. . . . Education and especially completion of primary schooling, must be a high priority" ("The Impact of Armed Conflict on Children," 1996, p. 14).
- *Help prevent future recruitment.* Most governments have adopted the Convention on the Rights of the Child, which prohibits the recruitment of children as soldiers. Communities and governments should be particularly aware of how children are recruited or forced to serve in military or paramilitary organizations, and intensify their work at the community and national levels to prevent such atrocities ("The Impact of Armed Conflict on Children," 1996).

Conclusion

While context has a tremendous impact on children's fears related to war and terrorism, other factors also make a difference. Temperament and age are salient contributors to what children fear and how they react to these fears. Chapter Three describes how temperament and individual child characteristics determine what children fear and how they respond to these fears. Chapter Four discusses how age also makes a difference.

References

American National Red Cross. (2001). *Helping children cope with trauma* [Brochure]. Baltimore: Author.

American School Counselor Association. (2003). *Deployment issues.* Retrieved March 1, 2003, from www.schoolcounselor.org/content.cfm?L1=1000&L2=103

Children and war. (1994). Retrieved March 1, 2003, from www.icrc.org/Web/eng/siteeng0.nsf/iwpList82/8EB73E21BBA6787CC1256B6600593731

Coeyman, M. (2001). Facing down fear: Lessons from city schools. *Christian Science Monitor, 93,* 14.

Crawford, S. (1995). Intensity and frequency of children's fears: Gender differences, ethnicity, income level (Doctoral dissertation, University of North Carolina). *Dissertation Abstracts International, 56,* 06A.

Honig, A. (1986). Stress and coping in children. *Young Children, 26,* 50-63.

Miller, M. (1997). Growing up amidst violence: Death anxiety, cognitive development, and conceptions of death in children (Doctoral dissertation, California Institute of Integral Studies). *Dissertation Abstracts International, 60,* 05B.

Moses, L. (2002). *The impact of socioeconomic status on children's perceptions, misunderstandings, and fears concerning the 2001 war on terrorism.* (Unpublished Doctoral dissertation, University of Alabama at Birmingham).

Schmitz, S. (1992). Three strikes and you're out: Academic failure and children of public housing. *Journal of Education, 174,* 41-54.

UNICEF, United Nations. (1996). *The impact of armed conflict on children.* Retrieved March 1, 2003, from www.unicef.org/graca/graright.htm

---

WEB SITES OF INTEREST

www.ppu.org.uk//learn/texts/convention2.html
www.ppu.org.uk//learn/texts/convention3.html
www.humanities.mcmaster.ca/peace-health/chasbush.pdf
www.unicef.org/children-in-war/machel/fact.htm
www.warchild.org/news/bull4/bull4.html
www.globalissues.net/guide/childrenandwar
www.warchild.org/
www.unicef.org/sowc96/16relief.htm

CHAPTER THREE
The Influence of Temperament on Children's Fears of War and Terrorism

Today is not a typical day at Meadowbrook Elementary School. A fire truck has arrived to extinguish a grease fire in the kitchen. Mr. Sanders's 4th-grade class was in the lunchroom when the excitement began. Bridgette was curious, as all of the children were, but she calmly followed Mr. Sanders's directions for evacuating the area. While Bridgette was interested in the fire and would share her experience with her grandparents later that day, she was not overwhelmed.

Paul had quite a different reaction. He was immediately upset and very concerned about the situation. Although he knew others would tease him later, he ran to Mr. Sanders, asking, "Will everything be OK? What should I do? Can I call my sister to come pick me up?" He was visibly shaken by this event; Paul does not adapt to new situations easily, and his immediate reaction is to withdraw or retreat.

Carla was intensely interested in the fire and ran into the kitchen to see what was going on. Mr. Sanders called her to line up with the other kids, but she was determined to see what was going on and intentionally ignored her teacher. When Mr. Sanders insisted that Carla return to the group, she replied, "No! I want to stay here. I'm not doing anything wrong. Leave me alone."

Bridgette, Paul, and Carla are all from comfortable, middle-class homes. None of them had ever experienced a fire before, yet each had a totally different reaction, as determined by their individual *temperaments*. Whenever a threat or a significant change in routine occurs, temperament makes a difference.

This chapter examines the influence of temperament on children's fears related to war and terrorism. First, temperament will be defined. Second, three temperament types are described in terms of how children of each type experience fear. The third and final section outlines ways to help children of each temperamental type deal with their fears concerning threats of war and terrorism.

What Is Temperament?

Temperament can be defined as the inborn part of one's personality (Hughes, 2002). Thomas and Chess (1984) proposed nine dimensions of temperament, and suggest that we are born with unique manifestations for each of the following dimensions: activity level, biological rhythms, approach/withdrawal, adaptability, mood, intensity of reaction, sensitivity, distractibility, and persistence (*Child Care Video Magazine*, 1990).

After identifying the nine inborn temperament traits, researchers began to notice that "certain aspects of these temperamental behavioral characteristics seemed to cluster together" (Hughes, 2002, p. 75). This grouping led researchers to identify three temperament types, which Thomas and Chess (1984) named **easy, slow-to-warm-up,** and **difficult.** Other names have been used. For example, *Child Care Video Magazine* (1990) refers to these same types as **flexible, fearful,** and **feisty**.

Temperament Types

The Easy Child. About 40 percent of children are considered to have an easy or flexible temperament (*Child Care Video Magazine,* 1990; Hughes, 2002; Thomas & Chess, 1984). These children have a positive mood and are generally quick to adapt to new situations. They have regular rhythms, and so are somewhat predictable in their reactions. Flexible children exhibit low sensitivity and low intensity. They have the same needs as other children. However, because they do not demand it, they may not receive the attention and support they need when fears arise. Bridgette is an example of an easy child.

The Slow-to-Warm-Up Child. Only 15 percent of children are considered slow-to-warm-up (Thomas & Chess, 1984). Children like Paul do not adapt well to new situations. Many slow-to-warm-up children fear the unknown, even when it turns out to be a fun and safe activity. These children withdraw and retreat. They are particularly vulnerable to all sorts of fears. When a threat of war or terrorism is present, the slow-to-warm-up child is terrified.

The Difficult Child. Ten percent of children are described as difficult or feisty (Hughes, 2002). A feisty child may be moody, active, intense, distractible, irregular, and sensitive (*Child Care Video Magazine,* 1990). Mr. Sanders was well aware that Carla was a difficult child, as she demonstrated many of these characteristics during the first week of school. Children who are feisty live life with zest and gusto and often get into trouble—especially during challenging times. Their curiosity and moodiness often seem to pose particular challenges for the adults who care for them.

Temperament and Children's Fears

In Chapter Two we discussed how context significantly influences children's fears related to war and terrorism. Context also makes a difference with temperament types. You may have noticed that the three temperament types described by Thomas and Chess (1984) add up to only 65 percent of children. What about the other 35 percent? Not all children can be categorized as simply flexible, fearful, or feisty. At least 35 percent of children exhibit characteristics of all three categories, depending on the context. Some children are flexible at home, feisty at school, and fearful of social events. The context makes the difference.

Conclusion

Both context and temperament are strong influences on how children respond to their fears of war or terrorism. Age also makes a difference. The next chapter explores developmentally responsive ways to help children deal with fears in times of war and terrorism.

References

Child Care Video Magazine. (1990). *Flexible, fearful, or feisty: The different temperaments of infants and toddlers.* Sacramento, CA: California State Department of Education.

Hughes, L. (2002). *Paving pathways: Child and adolescent development.* Belmont, CA: Wadsworth.

Thomas, A., & Chess, S. (1984). Genesis and evaluation of behavioral disorder: From infancy to early adult life. *American Journal of Psychiatry, 141,* 1-9.

Temperament and Fears of War or Terrorism:
Suggestions for Helping Children Cope

Ways To Help the Easy Child
- Observe flexible children closely. Because they do not demand attention, they are less likely to receive the attention they need during a crisis situation. Check in with them and ask them to tell you what they are feeling about war and terrorism.
- Set up a special time to interact with easy children. Both difficult and slow-to-warm-up children demand a lot of time. It is important to *make* time to talk to easy children. An interesting way for a classroom teacher to determine who the easy children are is to sit down once a month and write down the names of all the children in the class. Invariably, the teacher will not remember one or two children. These children may not demand teacher time, and thus do not make their presence felt. Nevertheless, these children need the same support as any other child.

Ways To Help the Slow-to-Warm-Up Child
- Assign one caregiver to act as primary support for a slow-to-warm-up child. Fearful children need one adult to interact with them when they are especially fearful, such as during the threat of war or terrorism.
- Provide a structured, predictable routine and environment. Since new things upset fearful children, they need stability and predictability. They need to know what to expect, especially when they are overwhelmed with fears related to their own safety and the safety of their loved ones.
- Be patient and don't push. In times of crisis, even at the level of a grease fire in the lunchroom, fearful children need patience. Their fears can be overwhelming or annoying for an adult who also must deal with the crisis. Remember, however, that slow-to-warm-up children are more likely to panic when they perceive that an adult is anxious and visibly troubled by a crisis situation. Fearful children often take their cues about how to react from the important adults in their lives.

Ways To Help the Difficult Child
- Be flexible with difficult children. Fearful kids who are feisty are more likely to "dig in their heels" when confronted with ultimatums.
- Use redirection. Rather than confronting feisty children's moody or intense reactions to fear, be flexible and redirect them temporarily. When the children calm down, take the time to discuss their fears.
- Prepare difficult children for change, whenever possible. In the vignette at the beginning of this chapter, Mr. Sanders could have dealt with Carla's behavior more easily if he had discussed beforehand what was expected during a fire. All teachers and parents will occasionally be caught off-guard. To the extent possible, however, teachers should discuss contingency plans and what is expected of the children.
- Provide opportunities for feisty children to express their frustrations in appropriate ways. Since feisty children have short fuses, they may need outlets for vigorous but safe play, or for physical activity that will help them safely vent their emotions.

[Adapted from *Child Care Video Magazine*, 1990]

CHAPTER FOUR
Age Makes a Difference

What kind of psychological price will . . . children pay for formative years in which a fireball of plane and passengers exploded within one of the nation's most triumphant landmarks, in which some of them missed soccer games or birthday trips to McDonald's because a man with a rifle was waiting to shoot passing strangers? . . . Most of us remember waking late on a crisp clear morning to blinding white beneath the window: no school because of snow! Now there are children who will remember school being canceled because of a rain of bullets. The new normal: a sniper day. (Quindlen, 2002, p. 68)

Age makes a difference when we talk about children's fears. Children cannot take care of themselves, and they know this. They need adults to help take care of them and provide a sense of security. Younger children are often confused when it comes to reality and fantasy, and so it is the adults in their lives who must protect them and help children interpret the world around them.

As we discussed briefly in the introduction, fears are quite common in children. Fear is a normal developmental reaction that arises as a response to a perceived danger (Smith, Davidson, White, & Poppen, 1990). This chapter is divided into three major sections. The first section describes the general fears of children that are related to age. The second part examines how children and adolescents react to traumatic events. The last section reports on children's fears specific to war and terrorism, and describes specific ways parents and teachers can help children cope.

General Fears of Children Related to Age

Children's fears are developmental. That is, children fear different things at different ages. Robinson, Rotter, Fey, and Robinson (1991) have compiled a list of some common fears of children between the ages of birth and 14. Their compilation was based on a synthesis of research reported by Croake and Knox (1971), Jersild and Holmes (1935), Kellerman (1981), Maurer (1965), Morris and Kratochwill (1983), and Robinson, Robinson, and Whetsell (1988). What follows is a description of Robinson et al.'s (1991) discussion of normative data on children's fears.

Children from birth to 6 months. Our youngest children often fear sudden movements and loud noises, and, in some ways, a lack of attention to their immediate needs. This stage of life is critical for developing a trusting relationship.

Children from 7 to 12 months. Stranger anxiety and separation anxiety are both characteristic of this period. Loud noises continue to scare children of this age group, as do large objects.

1-year-olds. Many children begin to develop fear of injury at 1 year of age. Children continue to work through stranger and separation anxiety, and separation from the parent, guardian, or caregiver frightens 1-year-olds.

2-year-olds. New fears emerge at this age as children begin to fear major changes in their environment, big animals, dimly lit rooms, and some machines and objects. Many are still afraid of loud noises.

3-year-olds. Three-year-olds are afraid of scary images. They also tend to fear masks, dark rooms, and snakes. Large animals also may seem frightening. Separation from a parent or guardian is still a fear of many children at this age.

4-year-olds. Many 4-year-olds fear the same things they did when they were 3. Noises at night can be added to the list of what many 4-year-olds fear.

5- and 6-year-olds. A change in children's fears appears to occur at this age. While children are still afraid of separation from parents or caregivers, a host of new fears arise that include weather-related fears such as thunder, being left alone, the dark, witches, monsters, ghosts, bad people, wild animals, and bodily injury.

7- and 8-year-olds. Being alone continues to scare children of this age. Seven-year-olds also may be afraid of kidnapping, being lost, storms, monsters, and the dark. Eight-year-olds tend to be more aware of "bad people" and fear robbers, muggers, and kidnappers, as well as guns, weapons, and some animals.

9- and 10-year-olds. Fear of bodily injury occurs during this age. Being afraid of bad people continues, and 9- and 10-year-olds may be afraid of strangers, bad dreams, and the dark.

10- and 11-year-olds. Fear of being hurt by another person is added to the fear of bodily injury during this age period. Bad dreams and being alone continue to frighten many children. Some children also fear tests, grades, and becoming sick.

12- and 13-year-olds. Fear of being taken away and hurt can be added to the list for this age group. Thoughts and fears of war also may develop at this age. Personal injury, kidnapping, and crime in general influence the thoughts of 12- and 13-year-olds. Grades, tests, and punishment remain concerns as children enter and continue through the middle school grades.

14-year-olds and above. Many adolescents fear sexual issues, personal relations, tests, and failing grades. Fear of war and anxiety about being alone also may be prevalent.

How Children and Adolescents React to Traumatic Events
According to the National Institute of Mental Health (NIMH) (2003), reaction to trauma can occur right after the event, or it may appear days or weeks later. Children exposed to disaster, tragedy, violence, or terrorism should be observed for signs of psychological distress. Children of different ages will react differently to a disaster. NIMH identifies the following age-related behaviors that may occur:

Infants, Toddlers, Preschoolers, and Kindergartners
Five-year-olds and younger may exhibit the following symptoms after a traumatic event:
- Crying
- Screaming
- Whimpering
- Fear of separation from their parents
- Clinging
- Frightened facial expressions
- Immobility

- Regressive behaviors (bed-wetting, thumb-sucking etc.)
- Strongly influenced by parental reactions to the event.

Elementary School-Age Children
Children between the ages of 6 and 11 may manifest the following symptoms after a traumatic event:
- Inability to concentrate
- Disruptive behavior
- Refusal to go to school
- Excessive withdrawal
- Regressive behaviors
- Nightmares
- Sleep disorders
- Irrational fears
- Outbursts and fighting
- Bodily symptoms, such as stomachaches, with no medical basis
- Failing grades in school
- Feelings of guilt
- A flat affect
- Depression
- Anxiety
- Emotional numbing.

Middle and High School Students
Adolescents between 12 and 18 may exhibit the following symptoms:
- Avoidance of reminders of the event
- Isolation
- Physical complaints
- Nightmares
- Flashbacks
- Emotional numbing
- Problems with friends or peers
- Depression
- Substance abuse
- Withdrawal
- Sleep disturbances
- Confusion
- Suicidal tendencies or thoughts
- Academic decline
- Avoidance of school and social activities
- Extreme guilt
- Revenge fantasies.

Children and adolescents who appear to be the most vulnerable and the most affected by traumatic events such as war or terrorism are those who have experienced a previous traumatic event, those who have suffered child abuse, and those with a history of mental health problems. Also, children who lack a strong support system, particularly within the family, are more vulnerable to these events.
[Adapted from "Helping Children and Adolescents Cope With Violence and Disasters," available on-line at www.nimh.nih.gov/publicat/violence.cfm]

Children's Developmental Fears Specific to War and Terrorism—Specific Ways Adults Can Help

In Chapter One, we described children's fears in general prior to a discussion of specific fears related to war and terrorism. In this chapter, we are taking a similar approach with regard to age. Robinson, Rotter, Fey, and Robinson (1991) have reported on children's general fears. How children and adolescents at different ages react to traumatic events was the focus of the previous section. Now, we will take a closer look at the specific fears at each age level that would be exacerbated by conditions or threats of war or terrorism.

Birth Through Age 3. Children from birth through age 3 will not understand the nature of war or terrorism. However, we know that they fear certain things related to war and terrorism, and that these fears will influence them whether they are directly involved with war or terrorism or they happen to see or hear about it in the media.

Some of the things children fear that are evoked by war include loud noises, sudden movements, strangers, separation, injury, the dark, and scary images such as masks.

How To Help
Children Birth Through Age 3

- *Avoid placing the child in front of the television during the news.* While very young children will not understand the dialogue related to war or terrorism, they will be afraid of loud noises, sudden movements, and scary images. The news during a time of war and terrorism is filled with such noises, movements, and images.
- *Provide the child with a daily routine that is stable and predictable.* Very young children also fear strangers, separation, and the loss of support. During times of war, routines are often changed drastically or become nonexistent. For parents and caregivers who raise our youngest children, however, maintaining a routine is a must. Many children have a parent, guardian, sibling, or other relative who is called away from home suddenly to military duty. Family routines change drastically, and fear and anxiety may sweep the adults who remain to care for the children. While children at such a young age do not "cognitively" understand what is happening, they are certainly "in tune" to the emotional atmosphere that surrounds them.
- *Make sure that at least one adult in the child's life is continually available for support.* As events often move quickly in times of war or terrorism, certain changes in routines may be unavoidable. Children need to feel supported and safe, and this need can be met by a stable, available caregiver, even when a change in rituals and routines is unavoidable.

Ages 4 Through 6. As we have noted, children's fears change at this age to include fear of bodily injury, bad people, monsters, being left alone, and thunder, while the children also continue to fear separation from parents or guardians. For children of this age, continue to follow those recommendations provided for children from birth through age 3 that are still applicable. In addition, the following responses are advisable:

How To Help
Children Ages 4 Through 6

- *Assure children that everything is being done to keep them safe and secure.* Since children of this age may fear bodily injury, bad people, monsters, being left alone, thunder, and separation from their parents, it is necessary from time to time to confidently stress that everything is being done to ensure their safety and security. During times of war, children are even more susceptible to fears, as they pick up on the anxieties and fears of their parents or guardians related to war and terrorism. The message of safety and security should be presented in a simple and reassuring manner.

- *Continually check on the images and messages the child is receiving from the multiple environments in which he navigates.* Children from 4 to 6 are transported from place to place throughout a given day. They may be in school or child care; at friends', relatives', and/or neighbors' homes; and numerous other places where people may not monitor the news media, conversations, or images that children of this age might encounter. Children from 4 through 6 often develop misconceptions about what they see and hear, particularly information related to war and terrorism. Therefore, it may be necessary to brief family, friends, and neighbors about what you know to be inappropriate conversations and images. Too often, inappropriate content concerning war and terrorism is discussed in front of children this age, which can lead to unnecessary stress.

- *Make sure that any changes in daily routines, especially with regard to parental or guardian involvement, are explained to the child.* Children this age continue to be afraid of being left alone and separated from their caregivers. Many parents or guardians have hectic schedules that prevent them from picking up their children at an appointed time. When situations like this cannot be avoided, make sure that caregivers reassure the child that everything is fine and that mommy or daddy will arrive, just at a different time. When parents/guardians do arrive, the child should be reassured emotionally more than cognitively. So, what does that mean? Children do not need a "cognitive" lecture about the reason that mommy and daddy had a schedule change. What children need are messages that the parents or guardians missed them, are happy to see them, and, now that they are reunited, want to spend time with them and enjoy their time together.

Ages 7 Through 9. Children in this age group may fear guns and weapons, accidents or bodily injury, bad people such as kidnappers, being lost, and bad dreams. Again, the recommendations provided for the previous ages should continue to be followed, in addition to new precautions for children ages 7 through 9.

How To Help
Children Ages 7 Through 9

- *Teach and encourage children to play cooperative games, rather than excessively competitive and/or violent ones.* Children of this age are now better able to take the viewpoint of another person. Cooperation, negotiation, and conflict resolution are important skills to learn at this age. Since children are often afraid of weapons and bodily injury at this age, be sure to monitor aggressive activities, video games, and television watching. Consider what behaviors might be learned from these experiences.

- *Listen closely to children at this age and answer their questions honestly, especially as they relate to war and terrorism.* "KidsPeace President C.T. O'Donnell II and the clinical experts at more than 50 centers across the country suggest . . . the following: [When] school children . . . ask, 'Can bad things happen here, or to me?' [do] not lie to [them]. Share that it is highly unlikely that anything like this will happen to them or in their community. Then reiterate how safe and protected they are by all those around them" (Kujawski, 2003, p. 1).

- *Talk with children about their feelings and the feelings they share with the important adults in their lives.* Discuss tragedies openly and honestly, and answer their questions as truthfully as possible while reassuring them (Kujawski, 2003).

Ages 10 Through 13. Every adult who works with this age group realizes this time of life can be difficult. Open communication is especially important between parent/guardian and child during this age span. In addition to school fears and anxieties, children from ages 10 through 13 are keenly aware of the possibilities of war and terrorism and fear being injured, kidnapped, or even killed. Some suggestions for providing support to this age group include:

How To Help
Children Ages 10 Through 13

- *Encourage parents/guardians to* "let [preteens] see your own feelings of grief, anger, and even fear. Your responses help [them] see alternative ways of coping with terrible tragedy" (Poussaint & Linn, 2003). While some adults might expect children this age to have an adult understanding of war and terrorism, they do not. They may be more exposed to and affected by media images and discussions of war and terrorism than younger children, as they have an ever-widening circle of influences. That is why it is especially important for parents/guardians to openly discuss feelings of grief, anger, and fear (Poussaint & Linn, 2003).

- *Look for signs of major behavior changes and seek appropriate help when necessary.* While this is true at every age, it is especially important for preteens. Worries about a new school, grades, extracurricular activities, and added stressors typical of this age range complicate a child's ability to cope with the unique concerns associated with war and terrorism. Parents and adults in many cases have become less central at this age and may be consulted less for advice and comfort. It is critical for adults to notice any significant behavior changes and seek help when needed.

Ages 14 and Up. The age of adolescence brings another set of worries. Sex, drugs, personal relations, popularity, and a host of other issues can be added to the list of concerns teenagers face. Adolescents' cognitive abilities have matured, and so they have many more questions about the possibilities of, and reasons for, war and terrorism. Further suggestions for this age group are noted below.

How To Help
Teenagers Ages 14 and Up

- *Encourage teenagers to discuss their questions and feelings about war and terrorism.* Parents should take the time to exchange viewpoints about armed conflicts with their teenagers. Teenagers are influenced by their peers and teachers, and can receive a lot of controversial and conflicting information about war and terrorism. Talking out their ideas, thoughts, and fears can help them clarify their thoughts on those issues.
- *Respect adolescents' differences of opinions and continually model ways to work through beliefs and fears about war and terrorism.* While younger children may take their cues from adults concerning war and terrorism, adolescents often have their own opinions, ideas, and fears that may differ from those of the important adults in their lives. Parents who are active in an anti-war movement, for example, may find their adolescent interested in joining the armed forces and going to war. Guardians who support a war effort may have a teenager who participates in anti-war protests. Open and respectful discussions about opinions, ideas, and fears can bring families closer together during a time of armed conflicts and terrorism, even when differences of opinion exist.

Conclusion

In the 21st century, the notion of ages and stages is much less popular than it was not that long ago. Educators, psychologists, and researchers have recognized other important factors that affect children as much or even more so. The two previous chapters described two of these influences—context and temperament. Chapter Five will examine how books, reading aloud to kids, and bibliotherapy can be used to help children of all ages and temperaments, and in all contexts, face the trauma of war and the threat of terrorism.

References

Croake, J., & Knox, F. (1971). A second look at adolescent fears. *Adolescence, 6,* 279-284.

Jersild, A., & Holmes, F. (1935). A study of children's fears. *Journal of Experimental Education, 2,* 109-118.

Kellerman, J. (1981). *Helping the fearful child.* New York: Norton.

Kujawski, L. (2003). *How to talk to kids about a possible war.* Retrieved March 1, 2003, from www.pnnonline.org/article.php?sid=4234

Maurer, A. (1965). What children fear. *Journal of Genetic Psychology, 10,* 265-277.

Morris, R. J., & Kratochwill, T. R. (1983). *Treating children's fears and phobias: A behavioral approach.* New York: Pergamon.

National Institute of Mental Health (NIMH). (2003). *Information about coping with traumatic events.* Retrieved March 30, 2003, from www.nimh.nih.gov/outline/traumatic.cfm

Poussaint, A., & Linn, S. (2003). *Talking about terrorism and war.* Retrieved March 1, 2003, from www.familyeducation.com

Quindlen, A. (2002, November 4). Young in a year of fear. *Newsweek, 140*(19), p. 68.

Robinson, E., Robinson, S., & Whetsell, M. (1988). The study of children's fears. *Journal of Humanistic Education and Development, 27*(6), 84-95.

Robinson, E. H., Rotter, J. C., Fey, M. A., & Robinson, S. L. (1991). Children's fears: Toward a preventive model. *The School Counselor, 38*(3), 187-202.

Smith, D., Davidson, P., White, P., & Poppen, W. (1990). An integrative theoretical model of children's fears. *Home Economics Research Journal, 19*, 151-158.

WEB RESOURCES
FOR TALKING WITH CHILDREN

http://streetcat.bnkst.edu/html/resources.html

www.childrennow.org/television/twk-news.htm

www.rethinkingschools.org/special_reports/sept11/pdf/911insrt.pdf

www.nasponline.org/NEAT/children_war.html

www.ppu.org.uk//learn/texts/convention3.html

www.apa.org/practice/ptresources.html

www.ag.uiuc.edu/~disaster/teacher/csndact2.html

http://home.earthlink.net/~dougyelmen/talk2kds.html

www.adc.org/action/2001/14september2001.htm

www.tolerance.org/teach/current/event.jsp?cid=247

CHAPTER FIVE

Using Children's Literature
To Make a Difference

One of the things people began to discover in the last century was that simple thoughts—just mere thoughts—are as powerful as electric batteries—as good for one as sunlight is, or as bad for one as poison. To let a sad thought or a bad one get into your mind is as dangerous as letting a scarlet fever germ into your body. If you let it stay there after it has got in you may never get over it as long as you live. *The Secret Garden* (Burnett, 1911, pp. 337-338)

Children's literature can be used as a tool to help children and young adolescents work through their fears of conflict and aggression. This chapter will explain the importance of bibliotherapy in the healing process, and the importance of reading aloud at home and in the classroom. Readers also will find guidance in how to choose and use books to help children work through their fears.

While childhood often is portrayed as a time of innocence, the harsh reality is that children experience fears—both real and imaginary. Child psychologists acknowledge that many adult phobias are rooted in unresolved childhood fears, and they warn that fears can intensify if not confronted during childhood. Therefore, parents, caregivers, and educators must not dismiss children's feelings, but rather acknowledge them and work to address them.

The Importance of Bibliotherapy

Reading stories about characters who are experiencing emotional stress and attempting to overcome obstacles can help some children cope with their own fears. Bibliotherapy can be defined as the use of literature to help children cope with emotional fears (Bernstein, 1989; Dole, 1990; Huck, Hepler, Hickman, & Kiefer, 1997; Norton & Norton, 2003; Rudman, 1995).

Four major coping strategies can be explored through bibliotherapy:

- Children who are introduced to storybook characters who experience worry, fear, or anxiety can relate those emotions to their own personal experiences. Through this identification, children realize that they are not alone in feeling the way they do.
- Children develop awareness that unsettling circumstances are not uncommon, and that wide ranges of emotions are normal and natural.
- The storybook characters illustrate ways of expressing emotions. Children can critically examine these models, and hypothesize about how to deal most effectively with fearful situations and reach an acceptable conclusion.
- In storybooks, the characters usually have the help of a friend or family member who supports them through difficult situations. By reading these stories, therefore, children learn the value of developing caring relationships with others.

Bibliotherapy can only be effective if the books are read in a caring and compassionate environment. The triangle of book, child, and caring reader makes a whole that is far greater than the sum of its parts. Both home and school offer natural settings that open doors to conversation. Fears cause children to retreat and resist reaching out to others; paradoxically, when children are experiencing fears, they need to bond with caregivers more than ever. Through bonding experiences, children's burdens become less heavy and troublesome, and they can find unexpected relief and peace. Reading aloud to children offers an opportunity for children to release their emotions and find renewal through interaction with the reader and with the text (Jalongo, 1983).

Loving home environments and caring classroom communities provide authentic contexts in which children may express their fears openly to others. Unfortunately, many children have limited support at home or in the classroom, and thus lack optimal opportunities to express and cope with their fears. When caring homes and school settings *are* optimal, they can provide the emotional support that children need when experiencing anxiety, fear, or emotional trauma related to the stresses of living in a world where war and terrorism are realities. The emotional aspects of reading aloud to children often offer the greatest benefit, even outweighing the educational value. Reading aloud to children certainly teaches the mind, and also teaches the heart and soul.

Reading Aloud at Home

While we could discuss at length the barriers many families face that make it difficult to spend time together reading aloud at home, our purpose here is to explain the tremendous benefits of doing so. The benefits to all children, especially those concerned with war and terrorism, make any effort to overcome the barriers worthwhile. While low-income families may lack resources and skills, and middle-class homes may struggle with over-burdened schedules, reading to children at home on a daily basis can make a tremendous difference to children, both cognitively and emotionally.

When a parent/guardian and child come to the end of a busy and hectic day, with the mundane responsibilities finally behind them, the time is ripe for emotional nurturing. Adults then can open the pages of a storybook and read to their children. Both child and adult will find comfort, love, and assurance through this activity, thus reinforcing their relationship at home and strengthening their bond. This special time of the day should be reserved and cherished. Reading together promotes talk between the adult and child and provides opportunities for close, physical and emotional intimacy with one another. Reading, talking, and touching work in concert to create a unique and pleasurable time for everyone.

Reading aloud to children should not end when the child has developed into a proficient reader. The value of reading to children remains constant across age levels. The educational, emotional, and social treasures to be found by reading aloud to children are waiting for the family. Just open the book and begin reading.

By establishing a regular time for read-aloud, parents/guardians can build a sense of continuity and security. Such a sense of security is critically important for a child struggling with fears. Furthermore, children are more likely to divulge their secret fears during the safety of the bedtime story hour. Even if the child does not articulate specific concerns, a perceptive adult will be able to sense a child's insecurities during this time spent in close interaction.

Many books for preschool and early primary age children address various emotions related to separation. These can be helpful if, during times of war or terrorism, caregivers are called away from home to serve their country in military duty. This is a family sacrifice as well as a personal sacrifice. The responsibility of parenting may fall on one parent, or on extended family members or friends. Children's feelings of insecurity are exacerbated by family separation and the threat of potential harm to the parent. During these times of separation, children from these families are especially vulnerable and need special support from caring adults (Heath, 1982; Hunter, 1982).

Caregivers fulfilling this unexpected duty must respond by offering an unwavering depth of compassion and care to the children. Segal (1986) emphasizes that maintaining family routines builds and sustains emotional support for the child. Continuing the bedtime story hour is an important way to respond thoughtfully and compassionately to the child's needs. The young child needs to know that she is safe, secure, and loved. Reading aloud books that portray the theme of reciprocal love between parent and child can affirm the caregiver's commitment to the child's welfare. Such books include *Baby! Talk!* by Penny Gentieu, *Guess How Much I Love You* by Sam McBratney, *First Steps* by Lee Wardlaw, and *I Love You, Little One* by Nancy Tafuri.

Literature is an important starting place for addressing the more subtle signs of fear that arise from separation. Overcoming the fears associated with starting school and the associated separation from home and family is a common theme in children's books, and one that young children can understand. Authors who write for young children often choose animal characters that have fears and worries similar to those expressed by children. In *Wimberly Worried*, by Kevin Henkes, a young mouse worries over big and little things. However, the start of school presents her with her biggest worry. In Kathryn Lasky's *Lunch Bunnies*, Clyde frets over all the things that could go wrong on his first day of school. This theme also is explored in *Off to School, Baby Duck!* by Amy Hest. In all of these books, the animal heroes face and overcome common emotions associated with new beginnings.

Fear of the dark, monsters, and things that go bump in the night keep many children awake. Tackling these fears are the subject of *Go Away, Big Green Monster* by Ed Emberly, *What If?* by Frances Thomas, and *Can't You Sleep, Little Bear?* by Martin Waddell. The fantasy genre can be very helpful for children dealing with real-life problems; nonfiction also is appropriate for addressing some fears. For example, in *Arf! Beg! Catch!: Dogs From A to Z*, Henry Horenstein uses humorous and appealing photographs to reassure children who are afraid of "man's best friend."

Reading aloud from many genres invites children to develop cognitively, socially, and emotionally. Set aside time each day and read with enthusiasm and enjoyment.

Reading Aloud in the Classroom

School is the place to continue the read-aloud tradition begun in the home, or a place to begin reading to children. Despite the overwhelming evidence of the educational value associated with reading aloud to children, many teachers neglect to do so or limit the time they spend reading to children. They often cite the demands of the curriculum and standardized testing as a reason for not including read-aloud time in their daily schedules. The importance of this time should not be overlooked, however. Although finding the time to read aloud in a busy school day is challenging, it can be eminently rewarding for those teachers who put forth the effort. Reading aloud to children can be the key that unlocks the mystery of reading for many children (Tunnel & Jacobs, 1989). It should be a vital and essential part of every school day, offering emotional as well as educational benefits to all children.

Choosing the Books

It does matter *what* we read. Teachers must be diligent in selecting the highest quality children's literature. Because so many excellent choices are available for read-aloud, the problem is not what book to use, but rather which one is best for the particular children in the classroom. The children's ages, their interests, and the purposes for the read-aloud should be determinants to narrow this search. Three highly acclaimed books that can help teachers sift through the many excellent choices available for read-aloud time are *The New Read-Aloud Handbook* by Jim Trelease (1989), *Valerie & Walter's Best Books for Children: A Lively, Opinionated Guide* by Valerie V. Lewis and Walter M. Mayes (1998), and *Read It Aloud!* by Monty Haas and Laurie Joy Haas (2000). In addition, the Children's Book Committee at the Bank Street College of Education publishes the useful pamphlet *Books To Read Aloud With Children of All Ages,* and it also develops an annual list of The Best Children's Books of the Year. Information on award-winning books also can be found in professional teacher journals, such as *The Reading Teacher* and *The Horn Book.* Libraries usually provide handy reference sheets listing those books that have received the highest awards given in children's literature. Ask the librarian for this list and for other book recommendations. Teaching colleagues also may be a source for reading suggestions.

Traditional Literature. Traditional literature is rooted in the literary heritage of all nations and cultures. Elementary-age children enjoy hearing tales of enchanted lands, supernatural animals, witches, magic, and fairy godmothers. Bruno Bettelheim (1976) convincingly argued that fairy tales are essential for children's emotional development, and that identification with the heroes of these stories helps children to deal effectively with emotional insecurities:

> This is exactly the message that fairy tales get across to the child in manifold form: that a struggle against severe difficulty in life is unavoidable, is an intrinsic part of human existence—but that if one does not shy away, but steadfastly meets unexpected and often unjust hardships, one masters all obstacles and in the end emerges victorious. (p. 8)

The presence of evil in the world is a reality, one that children are particularly aware of during times of war and threats of terrorism. In fairy tales, goodness and life overcome evil and death. The simple and straightforward themes and lessons found in traditional literature—evil is punished, love is merciful and kind, courage is rewarded, struggle for freedom is possible—can be very reassuring to confused and anxious children.

Biographies. Children who are facing fearful obstacles of any kind may find comfort in hearing stories about people who overcame insurmountable odds to achieve their personal goals. Narrative biographies appeal to children, because many of these accounts describe individuals who find in oppressive situations strength born of determination and courage, which helps them persevere throughout difficult times.

Children who have relatives serving in the armed forces may find comfort from books about historical leaders who also went to war. Reading stories about heroic figures allows children to think reflectively about their own lives, while learning about the history of the country currently being served by a parent, grandparent, sibling, or friend. Listed below are some notable biographers and some worthwhile books about individuals who struggled with, and overcame, adversity or fears.

Biographies

Notable Books:

Adler, D. (1989). *A picture book of Martin Luther King, Jr.* New York: Holiday House.

Bradby, M. (1995). *More than anything else.* Illus. by Chris Soentpiet. New York: Orchard Books.

Bridges, R. (1999). *Through my eyes.* New York: Scholastic.

Coles, R. (1995). *The story of Ruby Bridges.* Illus. by George Ford. New York: Scholastic.

Cooper, F. (1996). *Mandela: From the life of the South African statesman.* New York: Philomel Books.

Freedman, R. (1987). *Lincoln: A photobiography.* New York: Clarion.

Freedman, R. (1993). *Eleanor Roosevelt: A life of discovery.* New York: Clarion.

Fritz, J. (1991). *Bully for you, Teddy Roosevelt.* New York: Putnam.

Fritz, J. (1995). *You want women to vote, Lizzie Stanton?* New York: Putnam.

Golenbock, P. (1990). *Teammates.* Illus. by Paul Bacon. San Diego, CA: Harcourt Brace.

Golenbock, P. (2001). *Hank Aaron: Brave in every way.* Illus. by Paul Lee. San Diego, CA: Harcourt Brace.

Ketchum, L. (2000). *Into a new country: Eight remarkable women of the west.* Boston: Little, Brown.

Krull, K. (1999). *Wilma unlimited: How Wilma Rudolph became the fastest woman in the world.* Illus. by David Diaz. San Diego, CA: Harcourt Brace.

Meltzer, M. (1990). *Columbus and the world around him.* New York: Watts.

Meltzer, M. (1998). *Ten queens: Portraits of women of power.* Illus. by Bethanne Anderson. New York: Dutton.

Ringgold, F. (1995). *My dream of Martin Luther King.* New York: Crown.

Wells, R. (1997). *Mary on horseback: Three mountain stories.* Illus. by Peter McCarty. New York: Dial Books.

Wells, R. (1999). *Streets of gold.* Illus. by Dan Andreasen. New York: Dial Books.

Multicultural Literature. Children are the hope for peace in the future. Teachers can help build that peace by increasing children's understanding of other cultures and nations. One good way to do this is by reading multicultural literature in class. Good teachers embrace a curriculum that fosters constructive dialogue among groups. Multicultural literature offers opportunities to teach acceptance of and appreciation for others, and to see ourselves as others see us—to view ourselves as global citizens.

Schools in many countries are becoming more linguistically and culturally diverse each year. Children have a natural curiosity about the diversity in the world that shapes their classrooms and communities. Remember, however, that multicultural discussions cease to be authentic when they focus only on the five "f's"—food, festivals, fun, fashion, and flags. An important reason for including multicultural literature in the curriculum is to promote the following goals of the UN Convention on the Rights of the Child, as cited by Kobus (1992):

- Understanding and respect for each child's cultural group identities
- Respect for and tolerance of cultural differences, including differences of gender, language, race, ethnicity, religion, region, and disabilities
- Understanding of and respect for universal human rights and fundamental freedoms
- Preparation of children for responsible life in a free society
- Knowledge of cross-cultural communication strategies, perspective taking, and conflict management skills to ensure understanding, peace, tolerance, and friendship among all peoples and groups. (p. 224)

Books about other cultures are integrated into the other resource lists found throughout this chapter.

History and Historical Fiction Related to War. Studying the past can foster inquiry into how to live peacefully by providing insights into what has failed, what has worked, and what might be possible. Children can find it reassuring to read about how people coped and survived during times of uncertainty. Listed below are books for children about historical events related to war, armed conflicts, and terrorism. In addition, books about immigration and the immigrants' struggles can be found at the end of this section.

War

World War I:
Rabin, S. (1994). *Casey over there.* Illus. by Greg Shed. San Diego, CA: Harcourt Brace.
Wells, R. (1993). *Waiting for the evening star.* Illus. by Susan Jeffers. New York: Dial.

World War II:
Ackerman, K. (1995). *The night crossing.* Illus. by Elizabeth Sayles. New York: Random House.
Auerbacher, I. (1993). *I am a star.* Illus. by Israel Bernbaum. New York: Puffin Books.
Bitton-Jackson, L. (1997). *I have lived a thousand years: Growing up in the Holocaust.* New York: Simon & Schuster.
Coleman, P. (1995). *Rosie the riveter: Women working on the home front in World War II.* New York: Crown.
Greenfield, H. (1993). *The hidden children.* New York: Ticknor & Fields.
Lord, B. (1984). *In the year of the boar and Jackie Robinson.* New York: Harper & Row.
Lowry, L. (1989). *Number the stars.* New York: Houghton Mifflin.
Mataz, C. (1993). *Daniel's story.* New York: Scholastic.
Meltzer, M. (1976). *Never to forget: The Jews of the Holocaust.* New York: Harper & Row.
Mochizuki, K. (1993). *Baseball saved us.* Illus. by Dom Lee. New York: Lee & Low.
Mochizuki, K. (1997). *Passage to freedom: The Sugihara story.* Illus. by Dom Lee. New York: Lee & Low.

War

World War II (cont'd):
Novac, A. (1997). *The beautiful days of my youth: My six months in Auschwitz and Plaszow.* Trans. by George Newman. New York: Clarion.
Rosenberg, M. (1998). *Hiding to survive: Stories of Jewish children rescued from the Holocaust.* New York: Clarion.
Sacks, M. (1994). *A pocket full of seeds.* Illus. by Ben Stahl. New York: Puffin.
Salisbury, G. (1994). *Under the blood-red sun.* New York: Delacorte.

The Israeli and Palestinian Conflict:
Holiday, L. (1999). *Children of Israel, Children of Palestine: Our own true stories.* New York: Scholastic.
Sullivan, E. T. (1999). *The Holocaust in literature for youth.* New York: Schocken.
Volavkova, H. (1994). *I never saw another butterfly.* New York: Schocken.

Immigration and Immigrant Experiences:
Blos, J. (1994). *Brooklyn doesn't rhyme.* Illus. by Paul Birling. New York: Scribner's Sons.
Bunting, E. (1988). *How many days to America?: A Thanksgiving story.* Illus. by Beth Peck. New York: Clarion.
Bunting, E. (1998). *So far from the sea.* Illus. by Chris K. Soentpiet. New York: Clarion.
Cohen, B. (1983). *Molly's pilgrim.* Illus. by Michael Deraney. New York: Lee & Shepard.
Heese, K. (1992). *Letters from Rifka.* New York: Puffin.
Meltzer, M. (1982). *Jewish Americans: A history in their own words, 1650-1950.* New York: Crowell.

Poetry. Poetry is used to express the many moods of life—anger and fear, rejection and humiliation, joy and delight. The delight we found in the "Mother Goose" rhymes and jingles we read as young children gives way to pleasure derived from more advanced forms poetry. Poets can capture in moving and insightful ways the deep emotions we experience during times of war. Poems like "Life Doesn't Frighten Me" by Maya Angelou can lead children into discussions about how to confront scary things. What makes them feel scared? How do they experience frightening situations?

In 1977, the National Council of Teachers of English established an Award for Excellence in Poetry for Children, given for the body of a poet's work. David McCord, Aileen Fisher, Darla Kuskin, Myra Livingston, Eve Merriam, John Ciardi, Lilian Mooer, Arnold Adoff, Valerie Worth, Barbara Esbense, and Eloise Greenfield all have received this honor. These poets explore every emotion from fear to joy. We suggest reading and choosing from their poems to help children deal with their own fears and other strong emotions.

Using Talk To Make a Difference
Talk is a dimension of learning that often is neglected in classrooms. Mean-

ingful and purposeful conversations about books not only help children learn to read, but also help them learn to love reading. Talk builds a foundation from which deeper discussions can develop. Children are more apt to explore what the books mean to them if the classroom reading promotes talk about such meaning.

Talk about books allows each child's unique voice to be heard. As children discuss what they read, they delve deeper into the magic of how words touch us. Often, students who are experiencing fears concerning war and terrorism find they can express their fears more easily through the discussion of books.

Through discussions about books, children learn to actively listen to the opinions and reflections of others. Ideally, the listener is not a passive recipient of other ideas, but rather an active listener who critically examines, explores, and possibly reshapes her own beliefs based on insights to be found in the expressions of others. Collaboration and exchange of ideas gives students the opportunity to understand their personal responses to reading, while developing social sensitivity and genuine interest in others' understandings and fears. Over time, mutually supportive relationships develop that help children build trust, respect, and caring for one another.

Building Home and School Connections
Reading, listening, and talking about children's books are all powerful tools for addressing children's fears. Providing parents with a list of books to read aloud at home is one way a teacher can facilitate reading and talking at home. Parents or caregivers who spend one-on-one time reading with their children will open up opportunities for discussions about their children's fears, including fears related to war and armed conflict. Schools, nonprofit organizations, and community foundations may want to help families living in poverty by buying or supplying books and helping them with their own reading.

Teachers can involve parents in school read-alouds, by asking parents to read the same books and to talk with their children about them. A list of important discussion points raised by the teacher and students during classroom read-aloud sessions could be sent home. This also can promote interaction between caregiver and child. The questions should not be carefully scripted, but rather should center on personal beliefs and experiences and how they connect to the reading of the book.

Parents and caregivers can be invited to the classroom for book talks. Such an invitation sends the message to parents that reading is important, and it demonstrates how reading and talking build interaction.

Conclusion
War and terrorism are profound themes; often, caregivers and teachers confronting such issues feel fractured and overwhelmed, and they wonder how to help children deal with these issues. Reading books and stories aloud to children and then talking about these books can be a starting point in helping children cope with their fears in an uncertain time. Books offer many examples of real and imaginary people who experienced hope, determination, and love as well as suffering, injustice, and death. Some particularly useful books of this type are listed after the reference section of this chapter.

An extensive collection of quality children's books, at home or at school, does not guarantee children will confront their fears. More effort is needed. Only when teachers and caregivers engage children in meaningful talk about their reading are children likely to develop into readers who can confront their fears.

Using children's literature, reading aloud to children, and talking about books are not the only vehicles we can use to help children cope with their fears of war and terrorism. Aesthetic experiences provide opportunities for children to express their concerns through other media. These experiences are the focus of Chapter Six.

References

Bernstein, J. E. (1989). Bibliotherapy: How books can help young children cope. In M. Rudman (Ed.), *Children's literature: Resource for the classroom.* Norwood, MA: Christopher Gordon.

Bettelheim, B. (1976). *The uses of enchantment: The meaning and importance of fairy tales.* New York: Knopf.

Dole, P. P. (1990). *Developing resiliency through children's literature: A guide for teachers and librarians, K-8.* Jefferson, NC: McFarland & Company.

Haas, M., & Haas, L. J. (2000). *Read it aloud: A parent's guide to sharing books with young children.* Natick, MI: Reading Railroad.

Heath, S. B. (1982). What no bedtime story means: Narrative skills at home and school. *Language and Society, 33*(1), 49-76.

Huck, C. S., Hepler, S., Hickman, J., & Kiefer, B. Z. (1997). *Children's literature in the elementary school* (6th ed.). Boston: McGraw Hill.

Hunter, E. J. (1982). *Families under the flag.* New York: Praeger.

Jalongo, M. R. (1983). Bibliotherapy: Literature to promote socioemotional growth. *The Reading Teacher, 36,* 796-802.

Kobus, D. K. (1992). Multicultural/global education: An educational agenda for the rights of the child. *Social Education, 56,* 224-227.

Lewis, V., & Mayes, W. M. (1998). *Valerie & Walter's best books for children: A lively, opinionated guide.* New York: Avon Books.

Norton, D. E., & Norton, S. E. (2003). *Through the eyes of a child: An introduction to children's literature* (6th ed.). Upper Saddle River, NJ: Merrill/Prentice Hall.

Rudman, M. (1995). *Children's literature: An issues approach* (3rd ed.). White Plains, NY: Longman.

Segal, M. W. (1986). The military and the family as greedy institutions. *Armed Forces and Society, 13*(1), 9-38.

Trelease, J. (1989). *The new read-aloud handbook.* New York: Viking.

Tunnel, M., & Jacobs, J. (1989). Using real books: Research findings on literature-based reading instruction. *The Reading Teacher, 42*(3), 470-477.

Children's Literature Cited in This Chapter

Angelou, M. (1998). *Life doesn't frighten me.* New York: Stewart, Tabor, & Chang.

Burnett, F. (1911). *The secret garden.* Illus. by Tasha Tudor. New York: HarperCollins.

Emberly, E. (1992). *Go away, big green monster.* Boston: Little, Brown.

Gentieu, P. (1999). *Baby! Talk!* New York: Crown Publishers.

Henkes, K. (2000). *Wimberly worried.* New York: Greenwillow Books.

Hest, A. (1999). *Off to school, baby duck.* Illus. by Jill Barton. Cambridge, MA: Candlewick Press.

Horenstein, H. (1999). *Arf! Beg! Catch! Dogs from a to z.* New York: Scholastic.

Lasky, K. (1996). *Lunch bunnies.* Illus. by Marilyn Hafner. Boston: Little, Brown.

McBratney, S. (1995). *Guess how much I love you?* Illus. by Anita Jeram. Cambridge, MA: Candlewick Press.

Tafuri, N. (1998). *I love you, little one.* New York: Scholastic.

Thomas, F. (1998). *What if?* Illus. by Ross Collins. New York: Hyperion.

Waddell, M. (1992). *Can't you sleep, little one?* Illus. by Barbara Birth. Cambridge, MA: Candlewick Press.

Books for Adults About Children's Experiences With War or Terrorism

American National Red Cross. (2002). *Facing fear: Helping young people deal with terrorism and other tragic events.* (2002). Baltimore: Author.

Arterburn, S., & Stoop, D. (2002). *130 questions children ask about war and terrorists: Comforting your child in uncertain times.* Wheaton, IL: Tyndale Press.

Disaster through the eyes of a child: Urban expressions of the World Trade Center attack. (2002). New York: School Success Press.

Harwayne, S. (2002). *Messages to ground zero: Children respond to September 11, 2001.* Portsmouth, NH: Heinemann.

WEB RESOURCES FOR CHILDREN'S LITERATURE

www.ala.org

www.cbcbooks.org

www.reading.org

www.ncte.org

www.ala.org

http://hbook.org

www.ucalgary.ca/~dkbrown/usawards.html

www2.wcoil.com/~ellerbee/childlit.html

www.slj.com/

http://members.aol.com/Mgoudie/ChildrensLit.html

CHAPTER SIX

Using Aesthetics
To Make a Difference

The purpose of this chapter is to describe the value of aesthetic activities during a time of war and terrorism, and to provide ways to incorporate art and photography in efforts to help children express their fears. Throughout history, art has been a valuable means of self-expression. Art allows children to learn about themselves, others, and the world around them. They reaffirm their individual identities as well as important group memberships by using representations. Through art, children express their inner world, often projecting their emotional states into their products. Art provides opportunities for children to express their fears, nightmares, anger, confusion, and sadness (Althouse, Johnson, & Mitchell, 2003). During times of war and terrorism, aesthetic expression provides a critical outlet for difficult emotions, and thus can be a very useful coping strategy.

The Value of Aesthetic Activities During a Time of War and Terrorism
Increased intellectual functioning, longer attention span, enhanced creativity, and better emotional adjustment are all byproducts of pursuing art activities during a time of stress. Children's artistic products also can offer adults insight into what children are experiencing and, if excessive psychological stresses are portrayed, can help adults recognize a need for referral services.

Caregivers should pay special attention to exaggerations, distortions, deformations, overemphases, and continuous repetitions of images and objects created in children's art. Such characteristics can signal areas of emotional importance for a particular child or group of children. Similarly, the exclusion of objects or persons can be relevant to understanding a child's psychological functioning. Placement, color, and positional relationships are also important in children's artwork, and can help clarify children's perceptions, especially concerning issues of war (Fryrear, Corbit, & Taylor, 1992). Even though caregivers should not be expected to engage in art therapy per se, it can be helpful if they understand the basic elements of art therapy so that they can provide support for children and refer them to counselors or therapists, as needed.

During a time of war or terrorism, children are exposed to many disturbing images and conversations. Understandably, they will have many questions and experience many emotions. The closer to home the war is for children, the more questions they will have and the more intense their emotional reactions will be. Supportive caregivers will need to take time to talk to children about their feelings, and be alert to signs that children are experiencing nightmares, fears, regressive behaviors, diminished cognitive functioning, and/or sleeping and eating problems. These reactions are consistent with the presence of acute stress and posttraumatic stress disorder (PTSD). During these times, recreational and relaxation opportunities, including art activities, are important.

The caregiver must provide the time and space for such activities, and strive to create age-appropriate art experiences (Herberholz & Herberholz, 1998). Materials should be selected that are safe for children. In times of war and terrorism, caregivers should be prepared to deal with images, words, and movements that reflect raids, destruction, homelessness, death, burials, enemies, and other violence-related themes. Such expressions should not be judged, but rather acknowledged as important clues and messages concerning the children's thoughts and concerns.

Ways To Incorporate Art and Photography in Efforts To Help Children Express Their Fears

Aesthetic experiences are beneficial for daily use with children. Such experiences can be especially important outlets for children with family members who have been quickly deployed away from home for military service, or for children who have been exposed to direct or indirect acts of war or terrorism. In many cases, children may not be able to verbalize their feelings about the situation, and so it is important that the caregivers provide other opportunities, through art or other media, for the children to express their feelings and emotions (Klepsch & Logie, 1992).

Listed below are several key suggestions for using art with children who are concerned about war and terrorism:

- Children can draw, sculpt, paint, take photographs, compose collages, and create dances. Children may follow any art style, such as impressionistic, naturalistic or realistic, expressionistic, abstract, cubistic, or pop art. Also, children may choose from among different styles of artistic expression. Older children may choose to create humorous, cartoon-like, sarcastic, and/or political representations. Even though these styles may not be what others expect and even may seem distasteful, they can represent meaningful and relevant ways for children to make sense of their worlds. Acceptance, valuing, and questioning from caring adults is important during the process of creation.
- Children can take turns discussing their artwork and describing the images they portrayed. This is usually the time when the important catharsis will take place, as children verbalize their feelings (Oster & Gould, 1987). Adults and other classmates can pose questions and ask for clarification of the artwork, relate similar experiences and feelings they may have experienced, and offer emotional support. However, caution is in order. Children should not be forced to talk about their productions if they do not want to at this time. Caregivers can talk one-on-one with specific children, or set times when they will be available, in case children want to discuss their artwork privately.
- Expressions of fears about war and terrorism should not be posted or shown to others without the child's explicit permission. This art is different from other classroom activities. It contains very personal information about children's emotional functioning and, as such, must be protected from public scrutiny. At times, children may want to post their images of war and their fear of enemies; nevertheless, proper consent needs to be obtained to avoid the possibility of additional emotional trauma in the event of misunderstandings by viewers (Klepsch & Logie, 1992).
- Therapeutic art experiences can be either scheduled or conducted more spontaneously in response to specific needs of the children. The advantages of planned lessons are that adults can prepare for this event and

not be blindsided by the children's emotional reactions and their related need for support. Also, planning allows for other supportive adults to be included in the activities. Planned lessons are helpful if they are carefully constructed and implemented. Some children may not want to participate in the first or second lessons, but may join in the activity after they spend some time observing. Topics for therapeutic art should be derived from the children's expressions, needs, and experiences.

- Caregivers need to keep a detailed log describing the images and themes in the children's work. This record-keeping helps caregivers know what issues have been discussed and what specific children's reactions or comments have been. Also, adults can learn the key ways each child uses to express particular ideas or feelings.

The following media can be used to work through fears of war and terrorism through aesthetic experiences:

Sand Trays. In sand trays, children can manipulate miniature objects that represent soldiers, police, ambulances, and people. As they role-play, children's perceptions, emotions, and fears will emerge. Children can make compositions and describe them to adults. They can take photographs of their displays, which can be useful for subsequent discussions at home and school. These photos could be placed in the child's file or used by the same child later to make a collage. If sand trays are used, several should be made available so that more than one child can work with this media. Different colored sand can elicit more creative representations. With paper and pencil, children can incorporate written messages into the sand tray images. If a child wishes to keep his sand tray image for a while, it should remain untouched by other children or adults until the child lets the teacher or caregiver know he is ready to dismantle it.

Clay Sculptures. By incorporating different colors and texture into clay sculptures, children can create dramatic compositions. In addition, the sculptures could be converted into permanent items when hardening clay (or clay "that can be cooked") is used. Making plaster molds is another way to provide permanency (Schirrmacher, 2002). Caution needs to be exercised since molds become hot during the process. Two advantages of making permanent sculptures is that the pieces can be used as commemorative items, and they can be assembled with other pieces by the same artist to provide a more complete picture of the child's inner world.

Permanent sculptures are great healing tools, since they communicate a great deal about the child's progression through emotional or psychological states. They also illustrate the child's progress in using coping skills. Children can narrate their journey during difficult times, from beginning to end, through these compositions. The sculptures can be shared with other children and adults, and thus operate as initiators of conversations about war, terrorism, fear, empathy, grief, or heroism.

Clay sculptures often take several days to complete. Children should be allowed to work with them over a period of time; they should be the ones to determine when they have finished their creations. As with sand trays, taking pictures of the final product is important. The pictures provide another vehicle for later discussions. Children can take their representations in clay form home to their parents to promote family discussions.

Photographs. Photography is an excellent medium for self-expression; it reflects the tendency of children to think in images. Young children in particular may lack the language skills necessary to fully describe a situation (Fryrear, Corbit, & Taylor, 1992). When children select items, people, and scenes to photograph, they may be giving clues to the emotional states within themselves or others. These images can be used not only for self-expression, but also for language building when children describe the photographs for others. In addition, children can discuss what emotions, feelings, or memories the photographs trigger.

Photographic images can give children the opportunity to represent some things they may not have the ability to draw or otherwise replicate. They may know what they want to do, but lack the aesthetic or fine motor skills to do it. This medium can reduce the resultant frustration and give children a way to discuss more complex ideas in art form.

The photography activities can begin with a guided discussion around a particular theme, or they can be left entirely to the children's discretion. What is important is that their interests and motivations are followed. Children will need to plan the productions and discussions.

When children are involved in planning, it is important to discuss whether they can take a limited or unlimited number of photos. Planning reduces the amount of pictures taken and helps the children generate a preview of what they are trying to portray. Children may need guidance when selecting the items they would like to photograph. Items could be brought from home, found in the community, or made by the children especially for picture taking. Planning is necessary to maximize children's self-involvement and expression (Fryrear & Corbit, 1992). Clearly, young children will not be able to plan and implement activities at the level older children can, so adults will need to help younger children select pictures, take photographs, and assist in every aspect of the compositions and photography.

Polaroid photography has the advantage of offering immediate development of pictures, and children can serve as photographers of their own artwork and that of others. Photographs also have the advantage of including the people who created the art. Some teachers may encourage children to bring pictures of family and friends to class. Pictures of parents, siblings, or friends who are in armed conflict can be brought to school and serve as prompts for discussions about children's feelings for their loved ones. These pictures can provide great comfort to the child. Computer art programs also can be used to enhance photography projects.

Collages. Collages can be constructed with any number of materials, including paper, photos, newspaper, magazines, construction paper, pictures, and natural objects. Collage allows for absolute flexibility in construction and expression. As with any other form of representation, it is important to take pictures for later use or discussion (Mayesky, 1998).

Collages can be used in several ways. They can be a child-initiated or a teacher-facilitated activity. Teachers can select topics and guide the children into appropriate discussions. Collages can be constructed either individually or with a group. Group collages allow for collaboration in expression. Through group collages, children can express common fears, feelings, and memories associated with war and violence. When children elicit others' help and support, they gain an added interpersonal benefit. Children learn, once again, that they are not alone. Adults can encourage discussions about coping mechanisms as an integral part of these group projects.

Play and Drama. Play is another activity that can help children deal with the psychological impact of violence in their lives. Through dramatic play, children can explore war-related themes, roles, and emotions associated with death, separation, fear, shame, anger, guilt, and perceptions about the enemy.

During dramatic play, children tend to identify with particular roles through skits, manipulation of materials, scenes, and props (Similansky & Shefatya, 1990). Children construct their plots and carry them out until the theme is "drained." Children's dramatic endeavors are an important means for understanding their relationships with the themes.

Environments rich with props and materials for dramatic play are recommended. While it is not appropriate to have toy guns or plastic grenades available, children sometimes may make these on their own out of blocks or paper. Such make-believe is acceptable, because the blocks also can be used to represent other items that promote other types of play. Armed toys are questionable, as they promote only aggressive play themes. When war-related toys are used in sand tray play, the objects tend to be small and so children do not use them as extensively as they would if they were full-size representations. Playing with war-related representations helps children understand violence, war, death, and feelings about aggression and violence, and helps them integrate the concepts of power and control (Carlsson-Paige & Levin, 1990).

Adults observing children's dramatizations can gain a better understanding of children's thinking and feelings. Dramatic play also can be learning opportunities for children. During role-play, children may invent enemies and enemy-related behaviors. Attentive caregivers can use these scripts as questioning and redirecting tools. For example, if children are totally dehumanizing the enemy, a caregiver can ask, "Does the enemy have children? How will they feel if their mother or father is killed? How would they feel about the one that kills them? Does the enemy have an enemy? What makes someone an enemy? What are other ways people could act?"

By challenging the polarization of an enemy and the presentation of only negative traits for enemies, an adult can help children think. As children develop the ability to take different perspectives, they will develop the empathy and sympathy that are necessary for future social and emotional functioning. Role-playing is then used as a teaching tool, as well as a mechanism for working through fears.

Children can write letters to military personnel or their families as a follow-up activity to their dramatic play. Caregivers can help children write these letters to soldiers and families around the world and encourage them to express their concerns and hopes for peace and wishes for a safe return. It is important that adults facilitate these initiatives and encourage children to be supportive of people who are experiencing war firsthand.

As with any other media or activity, children should be allowed to choose not to participate or to stop the dramatic play when they feel the need to do so. Usually, they will stop when 1) they are satisfied with the process, 2) they have expressed all the emotions of the moment, or 3) they are frightened or becoming upset. Adult intervention is vital in the latter case to help children return to a more emotionally balanced state.

Other Artistic Activities That Can Be Used

Any artistic activity is appropriate as long as it is safe and secure for children of a particular age. The Arts and Craft Materials Institute has produced guidelines for safe materials for use by children. However, certain materials should be *avoided.* These include glitter, knives or sharp objects, electrical appliances such a glue guns, rubber cement, balloons, power paints, meat trays, toxic felt tip markers, enamels, and paint sprays (Herr & Larson, 2000). Talk to children about the proper use of such materials and supplies as staplers, tooth picks, and glue. Discuss possible problems with materials and supplies, and give direct guidelines as to their usage. Of course, aesthetic activities always should be supervised.

Some additional types of activities that children can engage in, either individually or as a group, include:

drawing and sketching	cutting
murals	tearing
object tracing	print making with objects
sandpaper art	marbling
sculptures	play dough
crayon shaving	painting with brushes and other objects
etching	texture painting with sponges
coffee painting	book making
tile art	paper making
paper folding	postcard making
dye making	

What Are the Main Goals for Using These Experiences?

Children who are concerned about war and terrorism need multiple opportunities and methods for expressing their feelings, thoughts, and emotions. The main goal of using aesthetic experiences with these children is to allow them a creative outlet, and to provide them with safe opportunities to talk about what may be causing them distress. Here are some suggestions for accomplishing this:

- Let children create and tell stories about their experiences and fears with war and terrorism.
- Help children understand that they are supported by adults and other children.
- Help children realize that everything is being done to make them safe and secure.
- Help children verbalize their emotions as they discuss their products. Ask, "How does this make you feel?"
- Help children understand that others have the same concerns and feelings they do. Let them know that they are not alone.
- Clear up any misconceptions the child may have. However, remember that many fears are irrational, and therefore cannot be mollified by mere explanation.

Conclusion

Thus far, we have considered how context, temperament, and age make a difference in how children respond in times of war and terrorism, and we have explored how reading aloud to children and offering aesthetic experiences can help children cope with their fears. In the Epilogue, we discuss the complexities and disequilibria adults face in helping children work through their fears of war and terrorism.

References

Althouse, R., Johnson, M., & Mitchell, S. (2003). *The colors of learning: Integrating the visual arts into the early childhood curriculum.* New York: Teachers College Press.

Carlsson-Paige, N., & Levin, D. (1990). *Who is calling the shots? How to respond effectively to children's fascination with war play and war toys.* Philadelphia: New Society.

Fryrear, J., & Corbit, I. (1992). *Instant images: Photo art therapy—A Jungian perspective.* Springfield, IL: Charles C. Thomas.

Fryrear, J., Corbit, I., & Taylor, S. (1992). *Instant images: A guide to using photography in therapy.* Dubuque, IA: Kendall/Hunt.

Herberholz, D., & Herberholz, B. (1998). *Artworks for elementary teachers: Developing artistic and perceptual awareness* (8th ed.). Boston: McGraw-Hill.

Herr, J., & Larson, Y. (2000). *Creative resources for the early childhood classroom.* Albany, NY: Delmar.

Klepsch, M., & Logie, L. (1992). *Children draw and tell: An introduction to the projective uses of children's human figure drawings.* New York: Brunner/Mazel.

Mayesky, M. (1998). *Creative activities for young children* (6th ed.). Albany, NY: Delmar.

Oster, G., & Gould, P. (1987). *Using drawings in assessment and therapy: A guide for mental health professionals.* New York: Brunner/Mazel.

Schirrmacher, R. (2002). *Art and creative development for young children.* Albany, NY: Delmar.

Similansky, S., & Shefatya, L. (1990). *Facilitating play: A medium for promoting cognitive, socio-emotional, and academic development in young children.* Gaithersburg, MD: Psychological and Educational Publications.

WEB RESOURCES FOR ART

www.papaink.org/gallery/home/artist/display/41.html
www.ag.uiuc.edu/~disaster/teacher/csndact2.html
www.cnn.com/WORLD/europe/9905/22/kosovo.children.art/
www.art-for-peace.org/pictures1.htm
www.afsc.org/ewnews/kosart.htm
www.anatomicallycorrect.org/stars&stripes.htm
www.healingthruart.com/exhibits/children/
www.usnews.com/usnews/9_11/articles/911psych.htm

EPILOGUE
The Complexities Adults Face in Helping Children Work Through Their Fears

*When supporting children during times of war and terrorism, the real challenge teachers and parents face is how to help children **over time.*** What we have described here is a Band-Aid approach. Band-Aids are important. They provide immediate support, but they focus only on the symptoms. A deeper look at the complexities involved in helping children face their fears over time is necessary. Certain unresolved issues emerge as we struggle to help children deal with their anxieties about safety in a volatile world. The interaction among context, age, and temperament is one issue. There are also five key tensions that adults face in assisting children in such uncertain times.

The Complexities of Context, Temperament, and Age

In Chapters Two through Four we considered context, temperament, and age as salient considerations in dealing with children's fears of armed conflict and terrorist activities. However, we described each one separately. In reality, the three interact. To discuss this interaction in practical terms, we return to the examples of two children described at the beginning of Chapter Two.

> Meredith lives in Thomasville, Alabama. Thomasville is a small town where over 1,600 residents were quickly deployed overseas for military duty. Meredith's mom, dad, uncle, and a cousin left quickly for military service, and she was sent to live with her aging grandparents in a neighboring town. This meant that Meredith had to transfer to another school where she does not know anyone. This was just the context; we did not discuss Meredith's temperament or age.
>
> In terms of temperament, Meredith is a fearful child. She withdraws and is slow to adapt if new challenges come her way. Meredith's immediate family has left quickly, she has moved to another community, and now she is attending a new school. All of her comforting routines have been changed or lost. To add to these challenges, Meredith is just 5 years old. According to Piaget, she is in the preoperational stage. We cannot help Meredith if we do not consider her context, temperament, and age simultaneously.
>
> Another child described in Chapter Two was Foday. He was kidnapped by the Revolutionary United Front (RUF) when he was 7. For eight years, he has served in a child army that has terrorized Sierra Leone. He has killed other children, cutting off their arms and legs with machetes.
>
> Temperamentally, Foday is a flexible child. He adapts quickly to what is expected of him. He follows orders and neither withdraws nor acts out. At 13, Foday needs to be removed from the RUF and re integrated into society. However, his parents are dead and there are no services to rehabilitate him and support his return to the community. In fact, the community from which he came is in turmoil and disarray.

In times of war and terrorism, it is the children who suffer the most. The problems of both Meredith and Foday are harsh, complex, and difficult to solve.

Five Tensions Adults Face in Working With Children's Fears

Adults face numerous tensions related to war and terrorism when striving to help children. Five of these are: 1) increased stress in children; 2) cultural, religious, and linguistic diversity; 3) continual threats related to safety; 4) simplistic ideas about what constitutes war and terrorism; and 5) overwhelming anxieties in adults.

Increased Stress in Children. From Singapore to the United States, children are victims of more and more stress (Sharpe, 2002; Stanford & Yamamoto, 2001). In many countries, the elementary curriculum is being pushed further downward, and so more and more is demanded of younger children. This comes at a time when children have increased fears of war and terrorism. Throughout the planet, life is stressful enough for children without adding the realities of armed conflicts and threats to their safety.

Cultural, Religious, and Linguistic Diversity. As a result of global migration, numerous multicultural societies can be found throughout the world. Diversity is valued, but it adds to the challenge of discussing war and terrorism with children. While we strive to teach respect for others and their opinions, we face more conflicting beliefs in our heterogeneous populations. Added to this complexity is the potential conflict between children who have parents or guardians in the military and children whose caregivers oppose war and/or participate in anti-war demonstrations. While no child or family member should be demeaned in any discussion about war or terrorism, conflicts of opinion are bound to emerge.

Continual Threats Related to Safety. Most resources related to dealing with children's fears about armed conflicts suggest we tell children that everything is being done to make them safe. Some suggest that we tell children that it is unlikely anything will happen to them. In this age of uncertainty, however, should we really make such a statement? Or should we prepare children for war and terrorism? Many adults are unsure about what the best approach might be.

Simplistic Ideas About What Constitutes War and Terrorism. Armed conflicts occur in all parts of the world. However, many adults focus on what the news media presents as the critical elements of war and terrorism. Many children of poverty live in war zones in their own neighborhoods. Gang fights, violence, rape, and murder occur on the same streets and in the same apartment complexes in which they live. Other children have parents or relatives who work in places of civil war, such as Colombia or the Philippines. Their fears and needs are as real as those who have caregivers in the Middle East. War and terrorism occur in neighborhoods, cities, and countries that are overlooked or minimized by adults and the news media. Expanding our understanding concerning war and terrorism is important in helping children and their families who live in dangerous environments.

Overwhelming Anxieties in Adults. Anyone who has been through an airport lately can attest to the fears and anxieties adults have about travel and their own safety. More and more uncertainty threatens the lives of adults who care for children in schools and/or have children of their own. It is the adults to whom children look for their cues, however. It is adults who model the coping mechanisms that children need to develop to build a sense of security. Adults must know themselves, acknowledge their own fears, and seek ways to work through them if they are to help children deal with their own fears.

Conclusion

Fears of war and terrorism lead us to an uncertain place. We live in that split second just before a frightened child begins to cry or a startled dog inhales to bark—unsure if we are being born or reborn, destroyed or transformed.

References

Sharpe, P. (2002). School days in Singapore: Young children's experiences and opportunities during a typical school day. *Childhood Education, 79,* 9-14.

Stanford, B. H., & Yamamoto, K. (Eds.). (2001). *Children and stress: Understanding and helping.* Olney, MD: Association for Childhood Education International.

AUTHOR BIOS

Lisa F. Moses is a recent Ph.D. graduate in early childhood education at the University of Alabama at Birmingham. The idea for this book was conceived following her dissertation research with young children concerning their fears following the September 11, 2001, attacks on the United States. Moses is also a recent graduate of the educational leadership program at the University of North Alabama. Her professional career includes classroom experience in 2nd, 7th, and 8th grades in regular education and she has taught children from every exceptionality category over her 20 years in the classroom. Moses has worked as a consultant for children with various disabilities in preschool special education and currently serves as a consultant for children who are visually impaired or blind. She has been actively involved in working with and for children who could become educationally "at-risk" due to some life circumstance beyond their control. These include children from poverty, grieving children, children with a disability, children traumatized by some life event, and children who are behaviorally challenged.

Jerry Aldridge is Professor of Early Childhood Education at the University of Alabama at Birmingham. He has published over 100 articles and 8 books. His publications include *No Easy Answers: Helping Children With Attention and Activity Level Differences*, 1998 (with Anne Eddowes and Patricia Kuby); *Current Issues and Trends in Education*, 2002 (with Renitta Goldman); and *Activity-Oriented Classrooms*, 1992 (with Milly Cowles). Jerry is a former President of the United States National Committee for the World Organization for Early Childhood Education (OMEP) and is the editor for the "Among the Periodicals" column in *Childhood Education*. His classroom teaching experience includes 1st grade, special education, and 4th grade.

Anarella Cellitti is a Master of Education in early childhood, minor in counseling; Ph.D. in early childhood; and a Master of Arts in Psychology, with emphasis in childhood trauma. She worked as a recreational therapist in mental health facilities, and as a therapist in private practice and in state mental health facilities with children and adolescents. In addition, she worked with school and mental health providers to help children make the transition from mental health hospitals to schools and communities. Cellitti integrated a team approach to serving children and families faced with acute and chronic psychological distress. Her work with mental health providers also has focused on recognizing and implementing culturally sensitive counseling strategies.

Gwenyth J. McCorquodale teaches children's literature to undergraduate and graduate students in the Department of Curriculum and Instruction at the University of Alabama at Birmingham. She has taught in the elementary schools of Georgia, Tennessee, Virginia, and Alabama. McCorquodale believes that meaningful talk about books not only helps students learn to read, but also helps them learn to love reading. Her research interests include integrated teaching, progressive education in the 21st century, and how meaningful talk creates classroom community.